The Relevance of Vedic Science in Hinduism

Sanskaaram

CONCEPTUALIZED BY: **Ar. K. SHIVKUMAR**

A Scientific Approach to
"Rituals"
The ABR Concept
(Act, Belief & Relevance)

Religion is meant to teach us true spiritual human character;
It is meant for Self-transformation; It is meant to transform —
anxiety into peace
arrogance into humility
envy to compassion
to awaken the pure soul in man & his love for the source, which is

"G O I

INDIA · SINGAPORE · MALAYSIA

ISBN 979-8-89067-661-0

DISCLAIMER

This book provides general informational advice and is not intended to replace professional advice. The author and publisher disclaim any liability for any errors or omissions in the content.

Readers are advised to exercise caution when applying the suggestions, as individual circumstances vary. Before making significant lifestyle changes or adopting new health practices, it is strongly advised to consult with qualified professionals, such as healthcare practitioners or nutritionists, to ensure the recommendations are safe and suitable for their specific situation.

The author and publisher are not responsible for any misuse, misunderstanding, or misinterpretation of the content and are not liable for any consequences arising from their use.

The book also emphasizes the importance of a holistic health approach, which should be undertaken under the guidance of experts to maximize effectiveness and safety. Individuals with existing health conditions or those taking medication should consult with their healthcare providers before making significant changes to their lifestyle, diet, or health practices.

INTRODUCTION

My inclined interest and fundamental knowledge of above areas accompanied with the hardcore experience related in safeguarding one's health during the on-going worldwide Covid-19 pandemic crises, enforced me to conceptualize the book 'SAPTAMSIDHI' dealing on varied Holistic Health approaches in sync with the Indian Vedic Culture and its impact and relevance in today's modern lifestyle. 'SAPTAMSIDHI'- being the principally conceptualized book, followed by other additional titles **"SANSKAARAM"**, PRANOYUGAM, AAROGYAVEDA, & SAPTAGYANAM.

SANSKAARAM being one among the other 4 more additional tiles of 'SAPTAMSIDHI, introduces the reader about Hinduism tradition & culture, Vedic rites & rituals in different stages of life and Relevance of Aum, Swastika and Bhagavad Gita, guiding us to understand the importance of Vedic Science in Hinduism.

A genuine attempt to unravel the principles behind the scientific Vedic practises has been sourced and outlined, so as to follow them in true spirit and not simply as a matter of customary tradition and experience its impact on our body, mind and soul.

Readers are intended to find these insights instructive and fascinating to enhance their beliefs and experience, the undeniably feel and its effects, in adhering to these Vedic rites and rituals based on Hinduism religion and culture.

An introductory basic information on Hinduism & Vedic culture and its practises to be adopted from sunrise to sunset and during major Indian festivals to enrich our lives with full of effective (instant-feel-so-good) positive vibrations.

This book acknowledges the basic Vedic cultural values and understanding of Nature's law and its Energy and subsequently living in accordance with it by performing small acts and routine practices, leading to a stress-free life without getting effected and infected by todays MODERN LIFESTYLE DISORDERS.

FOREWORD

FACULTY OF MANAGEMENT STUDIES
INSTITUTE OF MANAGEMENT STUDIES

Date: 07-01-2024

<u>FOREWORD</u>

It gives me immense pleasure to know that **Architect K. Shivkumar** has conceptualised the book titled **"SAPTAMSIDHI"**— the Principle book which is followed by its other supplementary titles 'SANSKAARAM', 'PRANOYUGAM', 'AAROGYAVEDA' & 'SAPTAGYANAM'.

The author has made a singular attempt in providing readers with a Reference Handbook for Wellness & Wellbeing that blends Ancient Practical Vedic Approaches for Today's Modern Lifestyle with advice on how to protect oneself from Modern Lifestyle Disorders through Prevention, Screening, and Treatment Measures.

Globally, there is an upsurge in psychiatric and lifestyle illnesses. I believe that these described and applied unique Vedic approaches and selected Yoga techniques such as Asanas, Pranayama, Mantras, Meditation, Mudras, and so on, when combined with the '7'- Seven different types of Holistic Health Approaches in sync with Indian Vedic culture, will provide a Holistic Treatment to cure these Modern Lifestyle Disorders miraculously.

This book's content will undoubtedly empower readers with a ready grasp of Hindu philosophy and profound information, helping them to live a healthier, happier, and stress-free life.

I truly think that **Architect K. Shivkumar's** book will be of great assistance to human society worldwide, and I applaud his efforts in creating an insightful and instructive work.

Prof. H. P. Mathur,
B.Tech. (IT-BHU), MMS, CAIIB, Ph.D.
Dean & Head,
Faculty of Management Studies, BHU.

Chairman, FMS/IM, BHU Placement Cell.
Director, Atal Incubation Centre, IM, BHU.
Director, Utkarsh Welfare Foundation.
Member, Board of Governors, UPES University.
Former Chief, University Employment Info & Guidance Bureau, BHU.
Former Coordinator, BHU Placement Coordination Cell.
Former Chairman, International Centre, BHU.

CONTENTS

1

AN OVERVIEW ON HINDUISM

Hinduism is a collective term applied to the many philosophical and religious traditions native to India. Hinduism has neither a specific moment of origin nor a specific founder. Rather, the tradition understands itself to be timeless, having always existed. Indeed, its collection of sacred texts is known, as a whole, as **Sanatana Dharma** -The Eternal Teaching.

It is thus a complex tradition that encompasses numerous interrelated religious doctrines and practices that have some common characteristics but which lack any unified system of beliefs and practices.

Hinduism encompasses a number of major sects, as well as countless subsects with local or regional variations. On one level, it is possible to view these sects as distinct religious traditions, with often very specific theologies and ritual traditions; on another level, however, they often understand themselves to be different means to reach a common end.

The Hindu worldview is grounded in the doctrines of samsara (the cycle of rebirth) and karma (the universal law of cause and effect), and fundamentally holds that one's actions (including one's thoughts) directly determine one's life, both one's current life and one's future lives.

Many, but not all, Hindus hold that the cosmos is populated by numerous deities and spiritual being-gods and goddesses, or devas-who actively influence the world and who interact with humans.

GENERAL FACTS ABOUT HINDUISM

- Total number of Hindus : **1.20 billion people**
- Original name : **Sanatana Dharma**
- Place of Origin : **India**
- Sacred text : **Vedas and Upanishads**
- Original language : **Sanskrit**

2

THE BASICS OF HINDUISM

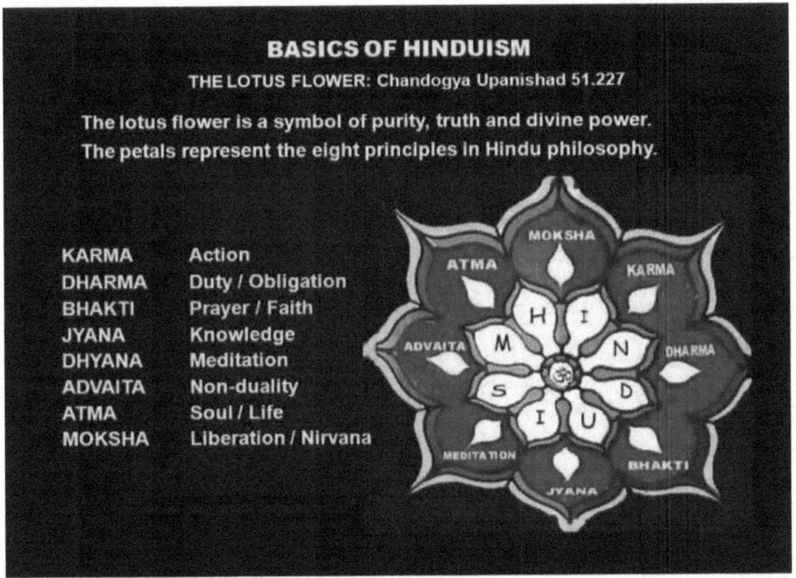

I) HINDUISM IS AT LEAST 5000 YEARS OLD

Hinduism is one of a few ancient religions to survive into modern times. The collection of traditions that compose modern-day Hinduism have developed over at least the past 5000 years, beginning in the Indus Valley region (in the nations of modern India and Pakistan), in what was the largest civilization of the ancient world. There is no 'founder' of Hinduism, nor single prophet or initial teacher. Hindus believe their religion has no identifiable beginning or end and, as such, often refer to it as **Sanatana Dharma** (the 'Eternal Way'). As for the name itself, 'Hindu' is a word first used by Persians, dating back to the 6th century BCE, to describe the people living beyond the Indus River. Initially it did not have a specific religious connotation. The religious meaning of the term did not develop for roughly another 1000 years.

II) THE VEDAS ARE ONE OF HINDUISM'S MANY PRIMARY RELIGIOUS TEXTS

Hinduism does not have a single holy book that guides religious practice. Instead, Hinduism has a large body of spiritual texts that guide devotees. First among these are the **Vedas** ("knowledge" in Sanskrit), a collection of hymns on the divine forces of nature presenting key Hindu teachings. The Vedas, considered to be realized (revealed) eternal truths, were passed down via an oral tradition for thousands of years before being written down. Hindu philosophy was further developed in the Upanishads. This philosophy was restated in the Puranas, the Ramayana, and the Mahabharata (the world's longest epic poem), as well as the Bhagavad Gita. Countless life stories, devotional poetry, and commentaries by sages and scholars have also contributed to the spiritual understanding and practice of Hindus.

III) HINDUISM IS ONE OF FOUR 'DHARMIC' OR 'INDIC' TRADITIONS

Hinduism, Buddhism, Jainism, and Sikhism can be referred to as the "Dharmic" or "Indic" traditions. The Dharma traditions share a broadly similar worldview, and share many spiritual concepts, such as dharma, karma, samsara, and moksha—though each religion understands and interprets them differently.

IV) HINDUISM SEES THE DIVINE PRESENT IN ALL EXISTENCE

The deepest single spiritual truth presented through the Vedas is that **Brahman** (roughly understood in English as 'the Absolute' or 'the Divine') pervades the entire universe. This divine reality, or its essential nature is present in all living beings, eternal and full of bliss. Brahman is understood as the cause of creation, as well as its preservation, dissolution and transformation, all done in a constant repeating cycle.

V) THE NATURE OF THE DIVINE IS UNDERSTOOD IN DIFFERENT WAYS IN DIFFERENT LINEAGES

Within Hinduism there is a broad spectrum of understanding about the nature of Brahman. Some Hindus believe that Brahman is infinite and formless, and can be worshipped as such, or in different forms. Other Hindus believe that the Divine is infinite and has a transcendental form. For example, some Vaishnavas believe that the one supreme form is Krishna, while Shaivites call this form Shiva.

VI) HINDUISM WORSHIPS THE DIVINE IN BOTH MALE & FEMALE FORM & ALSO ANIMAL FORM

Hindus believe that Brahman can take form, they accept that there are a variety of ways in which all human beings can connect with the Divine. This universal Divinity is worshipped in both male and female forms. The female form is known as Devi, which is a manifestation of Shakti (energy or creative force). Other forms combine male and female aspects together and some resemble with animal form, such as Ganesh or Hanuman. Each of these forms has a symbolic meaning. Hindus have long told stories about these various forms of the divine to inspire devotion and instil ethical values.

VII) HINDUS PRAY TO DIFFERENT ASPECTS OF THE DIVINE

Hindus pray to different forms of Brahman as manifestations of particular divine qualities or powers. E.g. Ganesh is honoured by Hindus (as well as sometimes by followers of other Indian religions) as the remover of obstacles and honoured for his great wisdom, and is often invoked before beginning any important task or project; Saraswati is the Goddess associated with learning and wisdom; Lakshmi is worshipped as the Goddess of Prosperity. God is believed to have taken human form of Rama to show people how to live the path of Dharma. Krishna is said to have come to eradicate evil and protect good. Shiva is worshipped as the lord of time and change.

VIII) HINDUS USE IMAGES IN WORSHIP TO MAKE THE INFINITE COMPREHENSIBLE TO THE HUMAN MIND

Hindus represent the various forms of God in consecrated images called Murti. A murti can be made of wood, stone, or metals (and sometimes can be naturally occurring, rather than fashioned by human hands). Murti offers a way to visualize and meditate upon Brahman, which due to its infinite nature is believed to be beyond the grasp of the human mind. Murti is often inaccurately translated as 'idol' but a more accurate translation is 'embodiment'. Hindu families conduct their daily worship at home altars and also at temples on special occasions. Many Hindus consult Gurus (recognized spiritual teachers and guides) for advice or answers to spiritual questions.

IX) HINDUS BELIEVE THE SOUL IS ETERNAL AND IS REBORN IN DIFFERENT FORMS

Hindus believe that the soul, **Atman**, is eternal. When the physical body dies the soul is reborn in another body. This continuous cycle of life, death, and rebirth is called **Samsara**. Rebirth is governed by Karma: the principle that every action (be it physical or mental) has a result, like cause and effect. What an individual experiences in this life are the result of their past actions, either actions they have already taken in this life or actions from a past life. How an individual acts today impacts the future, both in terms of effects felt later on in this life or in a future birth.

Though the effects of Karma make certain actions easier or more difficult to take, just as our personal habits influence our lives, this is not a deterministic or fatalistic system. Rather, we all have the ability to freely choose how to act in any situation.

X) HINDUS BELIEVE WE EACH HAVE FOUR GOALS IN LIFE:

- **Dharma** : Conducting ourselves in a way conducive to spiritual advancement,
- **Artha** : The pursuit of material prosperity,
- **Kama** : Enjoyment of the material world, and
- **Moksha** : Liberation from the attachments caused by dependence on the material world and from the cycle of birth and rebirth.

XI) THERE ARE FOUR PATHS TO MOKSHA

Hindu scripture outline four primary paths to experience God's presence and ultimately obtain the fourth goal, **Moksha**. These paths are not mutually exclusive and can be pursued simultaneously depending on an individual's inclination. These paths are:

- **Karma Yoga** : Performing one's duties selflessly
- **Bhakti Yoga** : Loving God through devotion and service
- **Jnana Yoga** : Study and contemplating sacred texts and

- **Raja Yoga** : Physically preparing the body and mind to allow deep meditation and introspection, so as to overcome suffering caused by material attachments.

XII) HINDUISM ACKNOWLEDGES THE POTENTIAL FOR TRUTH IN OTHER RELIGIONS

Hinduism is a deeply pluralistic tradition, promoting respect for other religions and acknowledges the potential for truth in them. Hindus see the varieties of religions and philosophies as different ways to understand and relate to God. This philosophy leads to pluralism within Hinduism and outside of it. The core philosophy of Hinduism is the search for truth, not the specific path taken. A quote from the Vedas that summarizes the Hindu perspective is, **"Truth is one; the wise call it by various names."**

3

THE BELEIFS IN HINDUISM

BELIEFS IN HINDUISM

Survey after survey reveals that more than 95 percent of Hindus believe in the existence of God. A broad set of beliefs stem from that most basic of beliefs, and they include the following.

- Belief in the Supreme Soul.
- Belief that Truth is the goal of life.
- Belief in the authority of the Vedas.
- Belief in the idea that time is circular and not linear.
- Belief in karma and karmic consequences.
- Belief in the concept of dharma.
- Belief in tolerance as the core value.

SOME BASIC HINDU CONCEPTS INCLUDE

- Hinduism embraces many religious ideas. For this reason, it's sometimes referred to as a "way of life" or a "family of religions," as opposed to a single, organized religion.
- Most forms of Hinduism are henotheistic, which means they worship a single deity, known as **"Brahman"**, but still recognize other gods and goddesses.

- Hindus believe in the doctrines of **Samsara** (the continuous cycle of life, death, and reincarnation) and **Karma** (the universal law of cause and effect).

- One of the key thoughts of Hinduism is **"Atman"**, or the belief in soul. This philosophy holds that living creatures have a soul, and they're all part of the supreme soul. The goal is to achieve **"Moksha",** or salvation, which ends the cycle of rebirths to become part of the absolute Soul.

- One fundamental principle of the religion is the idea that people's actions and thoughts directly determine their current life and future lives.

- Hindus strive to achieve **Dharma**, which is a code of living that emphasizes good conduct and morality.

- Hindus revere all living creatures and consider the cow a sacred animal.

- Food is an important part of life for Hindus. Most don't eat beef or pork, and many are vegetarians.

- Hinduism is closely related to other Indian religions, including Buddhism, Sikhism and Jainism.

4

THE SCRIPTURES OF HINDUISM

THE 2 KEYS OF HINDU SCRIPTURES

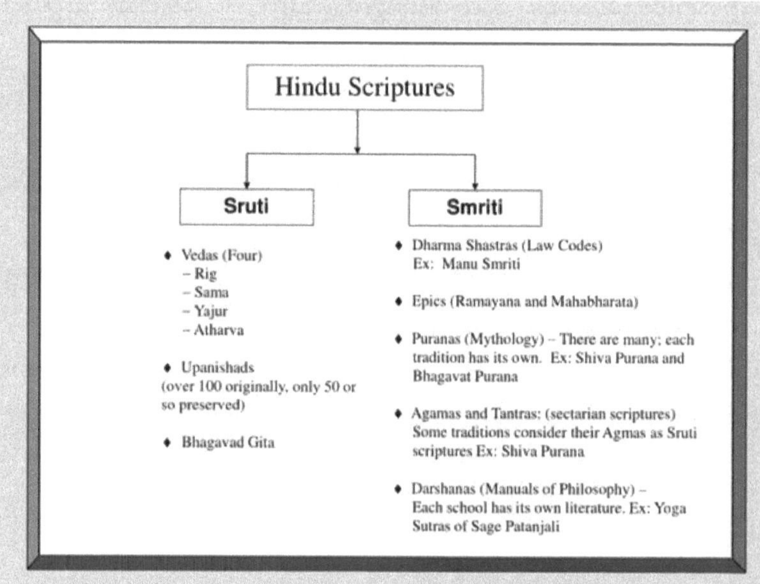

KEY HINDU SCRIPTURES

Hinduism is rich in scripture and includes an extensive collection of ancient religious writings. These sacred texts are classified broadly into two categories: **Shruti and Smriti.**

The word Shruti literally means "heard" and consists of what Hindus believe to be eternal truths akin to natural law. These texts are revered as "revealed" or divine in origin and are believed to contain the foundational truths of Hinduism.

The second category of scripture is Smriti, which literally means "Memory," and is distinguished from Shruti in terms of its origin. Teachings in Smriti texts are meant to be remind adherents the eternal truths of Shruti, and read and interpreted in light of changing circumstances over Kala (time), Desha (land), and Guna (personality).

THE MOST WELL KNOWN TEXTS INCLUDE:

SHRUTI:

It is that, which has been heard and is canonical, consisting of revelation and unquestionable truth.

Vedas: The word Veda means **"Knowledge"**. There are four **Vedas Rigveda, Samaveda, Yajurveda** and **Atharvaveda**, of which the Rigveda is the oldest.

Upanishads: These texts, numbering over 100, contain an extensive exploration of the methods of understanding the Self, God, and the Nature of the world.

SMRITI:

It is "that which has been remembered" supplementary and may change over time.

Upavedas: The Upavedas consist of four main texts, including:

Ayurveda	–	science of health and life
Dhanurveda	–	science of warfare
Gandharvaveda	–	the study of aesthetics, and delineates art forms
Arthashastra	–	guidance on public administration, governance, economy, and politics

PURANAS:

Stories in the Puranas translate the meanings of the ancient Shruti scriptures and teach them to the masses by explaining the teachings of the Vedas and Upanishads through stories and parables. There are 18 major Puranas (Mahapuranas) and many minor ones (upapuranas).

RAMAYANA:

It's a popular epic that tells the life story the noble prince named Rama, whom Hindus believe to be an incarnation of the

Divine. Prince Rama suffers year of exile and many hardships while destroying powerful demons before returning to rule his kingdom. There are numerous versions of the Ramayana, of which the most well-known are those by the original author sage Valmiki and the poet-saint Tulsidas.

MAHABHARATA:

With over 100,000 verses, the Mahabharata is a historical epic, and is the longest poem the world has known. Based on an extended conflict between two branches of the Kaurava family, the Mahabharata is a trove of stories and discourses on the practice of dharma, including the importance of truth, justice, self sacrifice, and the upholding of dharma, the need for complete devotion to God, and the ultimate futility of war.

BHAGAVAD GITA:

The Bhagavad Gita is a primary scripture for Hindus. Although it is a tiny part of the Mahabharata and technically classed as a Smriti text, it is traditionally accorded the rank of an Upanishad. It is meant to help one understand that upholding Dharma can be challenging, especially in situations where there is not a clear right or wrong.

AGAMA SHASTRAS:

Ancient and numerous, including many that have been lost over the centuries, these texts deal with practical aspects of devotion and worship, including personal and temple rituals and practices.

5

THE FOUR MAJOR TRADITIONS OF HINDUISM

Hinduism has many sects and is divided into the following:

- **Shaivism** - Devotees of God Shiva
- **Vaishnava** - Devotees of God Vishnu
- **Shaktism** - Devotees Goddess Devi
- **Smarta** - Devotees of Brahman and all major deities

The key concepts and practises of the four major denominations of Hinduism can be compared as below:

PILLARS OF THE BASIC TRADITIONS IN HINDUISM

Comparison Between the 4 Major Sects

SR.	DESCRIPTION	1 SHAIVA TRADITIONS
1	**SCRIPTURAL AUTHORITY**	Vedas, Upanishads and Agamas
2	**SUPREME DEITY**	God Shiva
3	**CREATOR**	Shiva
4	**AVATAR**	Major
5	**MONASTIC LIFE**	Recommends
6	**RITUALS, BHAKTI**	Affirms
7	**AHIMSA & VEGETARIANISM**	Recommends, Optional
8	**FREE WILL, MAYA & KARMA**	Affirms
9	**METAPHYSICS**	Brahman (Shiva), Atman (Soul Self)
10	**EPISTEMOLOGY (PRAMANA)**	1. Perception 2. Inference 3. Reliable Testimony 4. Self-evident
11	**PHILOSOPHY**	Dvaita, Qualified-advaita, Advaita
12	**SALVATION (SOTERIOLOGY)**	Jivanmukta, Charya-Kriya-Yoga-Jnan

2	3	4
VAISHNAVA TRADITIONS	**SHAKTA TRADITIONS**	**SMARTA TRADITIONS**
Vedas, Upanishads and Agamas	Vedas & Upanishads	Vedas & Upanishads
God Vishnu	Goddess Devi	None
Vishnu	Devi	Brahman Principle
Key Concept	Significant	Minor
Accepts	Accepts	Recommends
Affirms	Affirms	Optional
Affirms	Optional	Recommends, Optional
Affirms	Affirms	Affirms
Brahman (Vishnu), Atman (Soul Self)	Brahman (Devi), Atman (Soul Self)	Brahman, Atman (Soul Self)
1. Perception 2. Inference 3. Reliable Testimony	1. Perception 2. Inference 3. Reliable Testimony	1. Perception 2. Inference 3. Comparison & Analogy 4. Postulation, Derivation 5. Negative/Cognitive proof 6. Reliable Testimony
Dvaita, Qualified-advaita, Advaita	Shakti advaita	Advaita
Videhmukti, Yoga, Champions house-holder life.	Bhakti, Tantra, Yoga	Jivanmukta, Advaita, Yoga, Champions monastic life.

6

THE RELEVANCE OF "AUM" & "SWASTIK" IN HINDU CULTURE

THE FORM OF "AUM"

"AUM" is spoken at the beginning and the end of Hindu mantras, prayers, and meditations and is frequently used in Buddhist and Jain rituals as well. Aum is used in the practice of Yoga and is related to techniques of auditory meditation.

From the 6th century, the written symbol of Aum was used to mark the beginning of a text in a manuscript or an inscription. Aum Parvat, a sacred peak at 6191m in the Indian Himalayas, is revered for its snow deposition pattern that resembles Aum.

With its threefold nature, special shape and unique sound, Aum lends itself to a variety of detailed symbolic interpretations. The symbol of AUM consists of three curves (curves 1, 2, and 3), one semicircle (curve 4), and a dot.

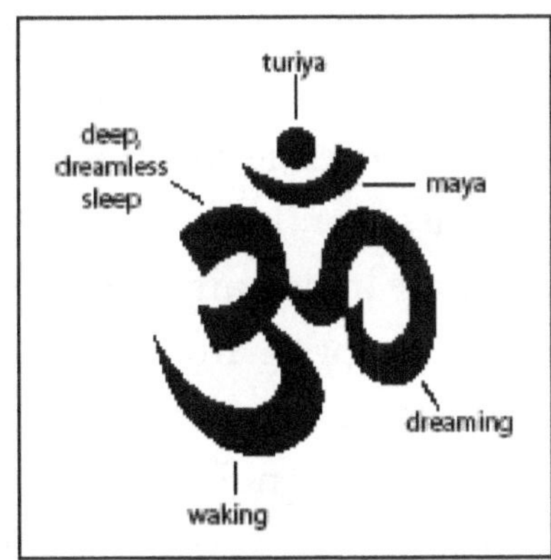

The 3 Curves, 1 Semi-circle & 1 Dot of Aum & Its Interpretation

1. **Jagrat** - (waking)
2. **Swapna** - (dreaming)
3. **Prajna / Sushupti** - (deep sleep)
4. **Turiya** - (bliss)
5. **Maya** - (illusion)

These stages of consciousness are visual but also are in sound. This is all represented in the symbol of "AUM"

The large lower curve '1' symbolizes the waking state **'Jagrat'**, in this state the consciousness is turned outwards through the gates of the senses. The larger size signifies that this is the most common ('majority') state of the human consciousness.

The middle curve '2' (which lies between deep sleep and the waking state) signifies the dream state **'Swapna'**. In this state the consciousness of the individual is turned inwards, and the dreaming self-beholds an enthralling view of the world behind the lids of the eyes.

The upper curve '3' denotes the state of deep sleep **'Prajna / Sushupti'** or the unconscious state. This is a state where the sleeper desires nothing nor beholds any dream.

These are the three states of an individual's consciousness, and since Indian mystic thought believes the entire manifested reality to spring from this consciousness, these three curves therefore represent the entire physical phenomenon.

The dot signifies the fourth state of consciousness, known in Sanskrit as **'Turiya'**. In this state the consciousness looks neither outwards nor inwards, nor the two together. It signifies the coming to rest of all differentiated, relative existence This utterly quiet, peaceful and blissful state is the ultimate aim of all spiritual activity. This Absolute (non-relative) state illuminates the other three states.

Finally, the semi-circle symbolizes **'Maya'** and separates the dot from the other three curves. Thus, it is the illusion of Maya that prevents us from the realization of this highest state of bliss.

The semi-circle is open at the top, and when ideally drawn does not touch the dot. This means that this highest state is not affected by maya. Maya only affects the manifested phenomenon. This effect is that of preventing the seeker from reaching his ultimate goal, the realization of the One, all-pervading, unmanifest, Absolute principle. In this manner, the form of AUM represents both the unmanifest and the manifest, the noumenon and the phenomenon.

THE SOUND OF "AUM"

AUM, represented by its symbol (the letter ॐ), is a combination of three sounds/letters – *A, U, M* (अ, उ, म).

Aum is considered the eternal sacred sound. It is the sound of creation and as such extremely powerful, infinite, and limitless.

It is also considered the bridge between the inner and outer worlds. Aum is Pranava, it is the root syllable (mool mantra) for all vaidik or tantric mantras. Aum is the reflection of objective realities.

It is both nama and rupa. Aum exists on its own, without reference to anything else. Mandukya Upanishad declares Aum as imperishable and everything (***Aum ityetadaksharam idam sarvam***) and uses it to explain Brahman as the ultimate reality ("All this world is the syllable, Aum."). Aum is the past, the present, and the future plus whatever there is beyond this three-fold temporal classification.

When one recites Aum, he/she speaks the universal language. It is a language that encompasses within itself all the languages of the world. When we utter a sound/letter, say vowel *A*, a specific part of the human vocal organ is activated.

When we recite Aum, the entire vocal organ is activated.

Aum is a combination of three sounds/letters – ***a, u, m*** (अ, उ, म) – and together they represent the universal Brahman. While pronouncing अ, the most interior (back) part of the open, mouth is used.

अ is also the first letter of the alphabet and is inherently present in all sounds produced by human speech organs. Next up, उ is pronounced from middle to front part.

Finally, with the pronunciation of म sound, the most frontal part of our vocal organ (lips) is used, resulting finally in the closing of the vocal cord. It is also the last letter of the alphabet in a sequence of one line.

As such, the pronunciation of ॐ is an invocation of the complete alphabet and hence perceptively all possible sounds. Hence, by pronouncing all three sounds अ, उ, म at once in the syllable ॐ, one is able to activate the entire spectrum of the human vocal cord – from the back of the mouth to the middle and front.

- "When we chant Aum, we are really singing a three-part sound: AUM, Ah…oooh…Mmm.
- Each part vibrates in a different part of the body and represents a different state of consciousness.
- The **Ah blooms** in the lower abdomen and represents Jagrat, the waking state.
- **Oooh vibrates** in the solar plexus and heart and represents Swapna, the dream state.
- **Mmm occurs** when we put our lips together, sending the vibrations into our skulls.
- With this sound we are calling to our awareness of Sushupti - deep sleep. And finally, Turiya exists in the continuing vibration, resonating, unstuck sound of Aum.

The threefold symbolism of AUM is comprehensible to the most 'ordinary' of us humans, realizable both on the intuitive and objective level. This is responsible for its widespread popularity and acceptance. That this symbolism extends over the entire spectrum of the manifested universe makes it a veritable font of spirituality.

THE 4 STATES OF HUMAN CONCIOUSNESS ON "AUM" RECITATION

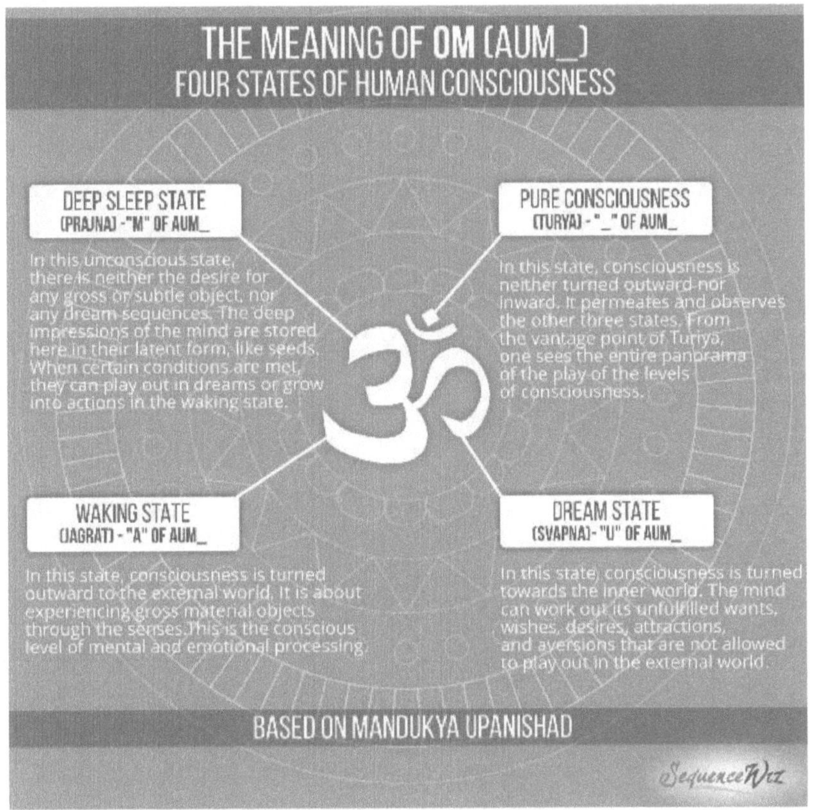

THE FORM OF "SWASTIKA"

The Form & Relevance of Swastika According to Satya Sanatana Dharma

According to Purusharth - KARMA means -
1. DHARAM
2. ARTH
3. KAAM
4. MOKSH

To attain "MOKSH" - the four ways of MUKTI are
1. SALAUKYA
2. SAMIPYAH
3. SARUPYAH
4. SAYUJIHA

The 4 ANTHAKARAN - Our Mind's decision
1. MAAN
2. BUDDHI
3. AHANKAAR
4. CHITTH

The 4 Pillars of "BHAKTI" - the centre circles
1. SHRADDHA.
2. VISHWAS
3. PREM
4. SAMARPAN

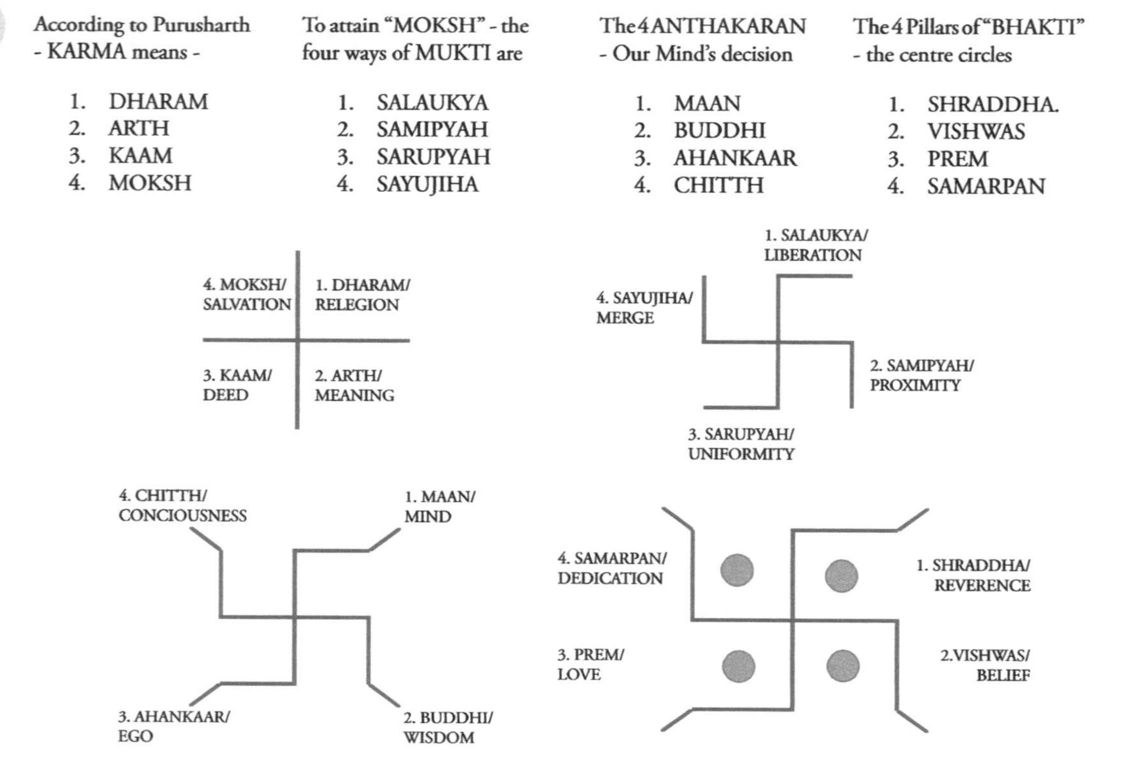

No Lines are crossing each other and all 16 Indriyaas meet at the cente i.e. BRAHMANSTHAAN, forming a complete symbol known as "SWASTIKA".

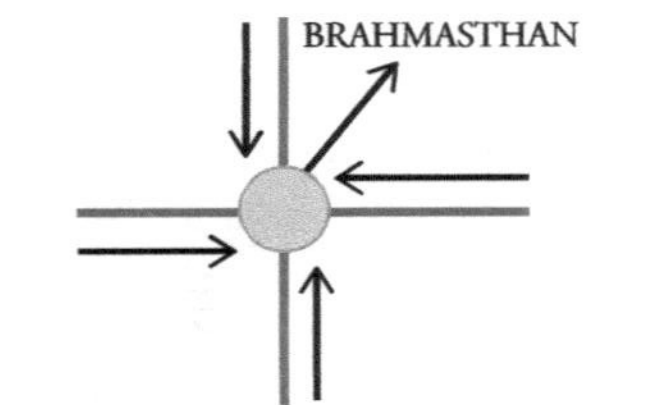

4 Arrows of PURUSHARTH - Horizontal lines directing towards BRAHMASTHAN

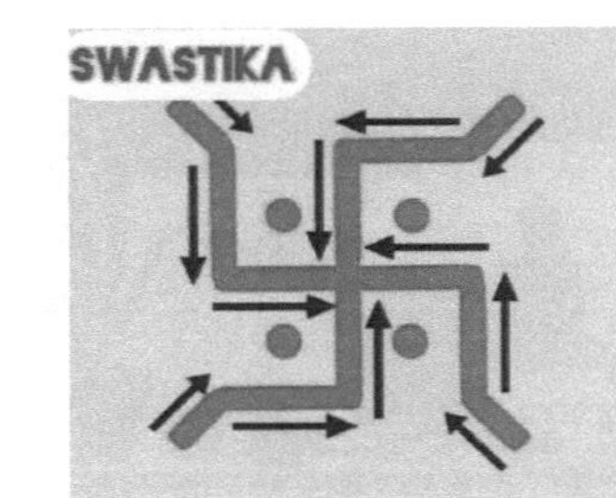

4 Arrows of MUKTI - Vertical and Horizontal arrows directing towards BRAHMASTHAN

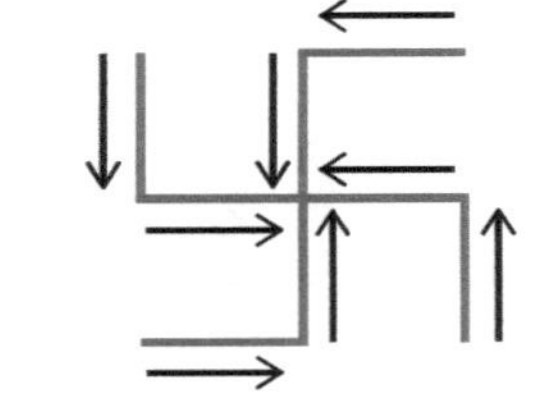

4 Arrows of ANTHAKARAN - inclined 45* arrows directing towards BRAHMASTHAN

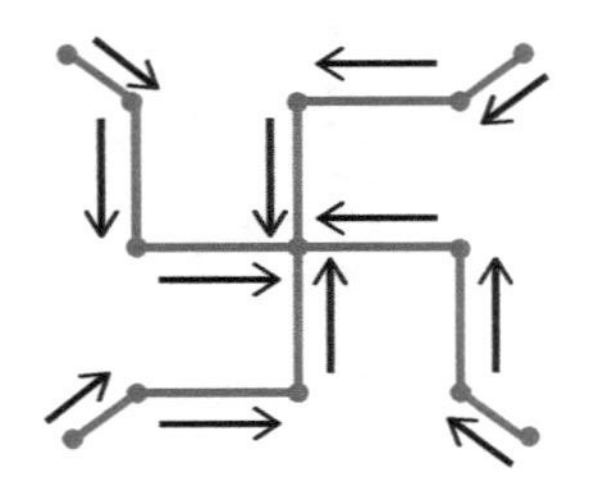

All arrows are directly meeting at "BRAHMASTHAN"

THE CONCLUSION : When all the 16 INDRIYAS converge at a central point i.e. BRAHMASTHAN and all their energies are centralised and directed to BRAHMASTHAN, then the overall effect creates a Multiple effects of Positive Energies.

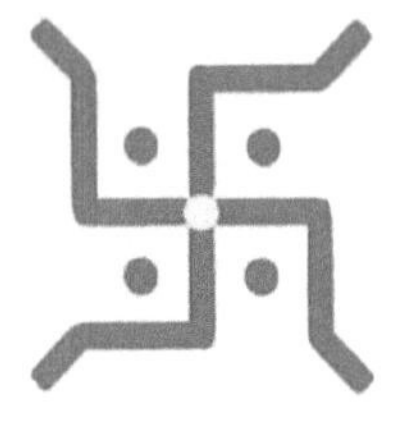 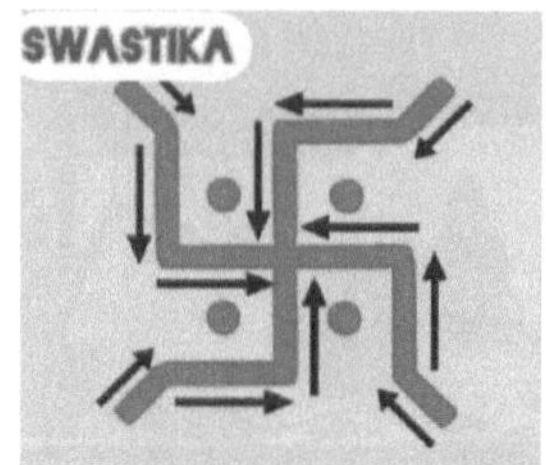

ORIGIN

The word Swastik has a definite etymological origin in Sanskrit. It is derived from the roots 'su' – meaning well or auspicious and 'as meaning' being.

Su asti yena tat swastikam

Swastik is that symbol through which everything auspicious occurs.

Scholars believe the word's origin in the Vedas, known as the Swasti mantra.

SWASTIKA IN RITUALS

1. Being an auspicious symbol with such inherently profound sentiments, the swastika is used during puja rites and rituals by Hindus.

   They imprint this using dry or wet kumkum on new articles, appliances, vehicles, the entrance of new business premises or home, etc.

   The underlying sentiment is that "let the article (being offered pujan) be redemptive (kalyankari) in life, not only for a mundane purpose but also to aid one on the spiritual path, towards moksha".

This is in consonance with Sanatan Dharma's idea of attaining the four endeavours (purusharthas) of life; dharma, artha, kama and moksha.

2. The swastika symbolizes mangalya – auspiciousness, peace, harmony and success in all ventures embarked upon in life.

3. Swastik is a symbolic form of Aum-kar.

4. It is a symbol of sacredness that wards off evil elements and herald's good fortune.

5. Swastik is imprinted on doorways of houses and ingrained in the flooring of mandirs as a symbolic form of auspiciousness.

6. It depicts; Surya, the "wheel of life" and four directions.

7. In India, the swastika has eternally embodied in sentiments, likewise:

    a. Kalyan (ultimate liberation) – swasti – auspicious, kalyan, ka – doer – one that bestows kalyan

    b. Man's quest to attain spiritual knowledge

    c. Prayer on behalf of all jivas for moksha

    d. Encompasses the whole cosmos.

    e. A symbol of Lakshmi – devi of wealth.

    f. A symbol of Vishnu. Its four bars represent Vishnu's four hands and Vishnu is the protector of the four directions (Vishnu Purana)

    g. Protection from the four directions.

    h. The symbol representing Sanatan Dharma and its sentiment of peace and moksha for all mankind.

7

THE RELEVANCE OF YOGA IN HINDUISM

THE MEANING AND PURPOSE OF YOGA

Yoga means a state or condition, a technique, auspiciousness and union. Patanjali defined yoga as the cessation of the modifications of the mind. The practice of yoga leads to mental stability, equanimity, concentration, meditation, good health, supernatural powers, devotion, self-transformation and liberation.

All the chapters in the Bhagavad Gita contain the word yoga, signifying its importance in Hinduism and in achieving liberation. Yoga is the means and yoga is also the goal. Through the practice of yoga you reach the highest state of yoga, which is union with your Inner Self or with the Supreme Self.

Yoga is a multidisciplinary tool extremely useful to purify the mind and body and gain control over our minds and emotions. Yoga is also the most popular means for self-transformation and physical wellbeing.

It is useful for both the wordily people seeking mental peace and ascetics seeking liberation. Yoga helps to become a better person, a better human being and a better devotee.

The most popular forms of yoga are classical yoga of Patanjali, also known as Ashtanga yoga, karma yoga, jnana yoga and bhakti yoga. Some Saiva traditions practice hatha yoga, mantra yoga and tantra yoga.

Inherent to all these yogas are sanyasa-yoga (the yoga of renunciation) and buddhi yoga (the yoga of one pointed intelligence). Yoga is an ancient ascetic practice which is mentioned and defined in several early Upanishads such as the Katha Upanishads. Besides there are several Yoga Upanishads which are exclusively devoted to its practice.

Yoga is the gift of Hinduism to the world. Yoga is practiced in other religions also, such as Buddhism, Jainism and Sikhism. But it is essentially a Hindu practice whose origins are rooted in the Vedas, more especially in the Upanishads.

WHAT DOES YOGA MEAN IN HINDUISM?

In Hinduism yoga is a way to attain self-realization and become one with God, or moksha. Yoga is a way to realize one's true self and connect the body, breath, mind, subconscious, conscious, and soul. It means uniting with the self.

Most of the yoga practiced in the west is actually not even yoga but just asana. Asana is the physical part of yoga, the stretches. In no way are the words yoga and asana interchangeable, and using them as such is cultural appropriation. True yoga itself is more of a lifestyle, with its most common form having 8 stages. The stages are listed below in another very helpful infographic

THE PYRAMID OF "YOGIC LIFE" - LEADING TO SELF REALIZATION AS PER YOGA CULTURE IN HINDUISM

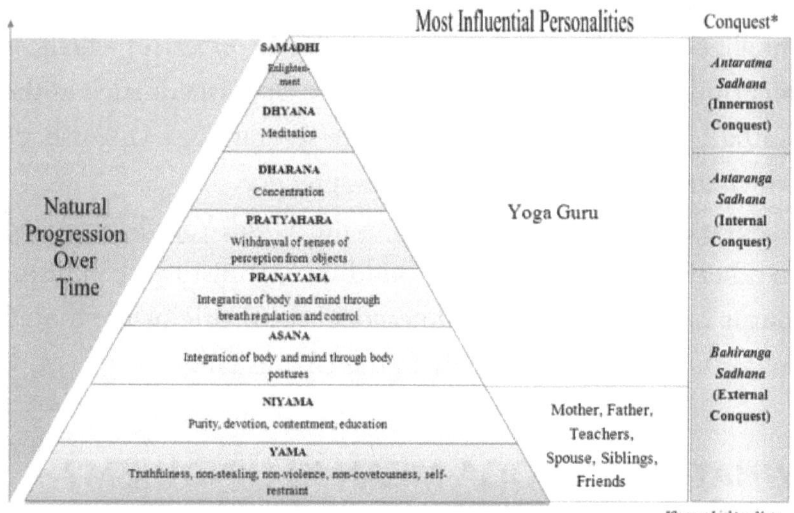

PATANJALI'S YOGA SUTRA IS AN AGE-OLD SCRIPTURE, A COLLECTION OF 196 INDIAN SUTRAS THAT EXPLAIN THE YOGIC PHILOSOPHY ON HOW TO LIVE LIFE AND WALK THE PATH OF SELF-REALIZATION.

The ancient sage Patanjali describes the yogic path to self-realization as **Ashtanga (अष्टाङ्ग),** or eight limbs:

- *ashta* = eight
- *anga* = limb

The second chapter, Sadhana-Pada, explains the aspects of the eightfold path and some of the motivations to live this way of life.

Sutra 2.28 | योगाङ्गानुष्ठानादशुद्धिक्षये ज्ञानदीप्तिराविवेकख्यातेः

yoga-anga-anusthanad-asuddhi-ksaye jnana-diptir-a-viveka-khyateh.

MEANING: By practicing the limbs of yoga, impurity is destroyed and the radiance of jnana (wisdom) leads to viveka (discernment).

Sutra 2.29 | यम नियमाअसन प्राणायाम प्रत्याहार धारणा ध्यान समाधयोऽष्टावङ्गानिः

yama-niyama-asana-pranayama-pratyahara-dharana-dyana-samadhayo stav-angani.

MEANING: The eight limbs of yoga are: yama, niyama, asana, pranayama, pratyahara, dharana, dhyana, and samadhi. These limbs are sequential steps on the path to enlightenment through yoga.

1. YAMA (SELF-RESTRAINT)

The first limb, *yama*, explains the codes of ethical behavior and how we conduct ourselves in life. Yama remind us of our responsibilities as social beings and has 5 principles:

- **Ahimsa** : nonviolence to ourselves and others
- **Satya** : truthfulness
- **Asteya** : non-stealing
- **Brahmacharya** : chastity
- **Aparigraha** : freedom from desire

2. NIYAMA (RIGHT OBSERVANCE)

The second limb, *niyama*, prescribes the self-discipline that moulds our morality and behavior. This code of conduct has 5 principles:

- **Saucha** : cleanliness
- **Santosa** : contentment
- **Tapas** : austerity
- **Svadhyaya** : study of one's own self including body, mind, intellect, and ego
- **Isvara Pranidhana** : devotion

3. ASANA (RIGHT ALIGNMENT)

Most of the world understands yoga as primarily as the physical practice of asanas. In Patanjali's Eightfold Path, we practice asana to deepen our ability to meditate, concentrate, and ultimately achieve Samadhi.

The third limb, *asana* (as = to sit), is where we develop the habit of discipline and the ability to concentrate.

Through a steady and comfortable sitting position, Patanjali describes that we loosen the tension in our bodies allowing us to merge our attention with the infinite.

Sutra 2.46 | स्थिरसुखमासनम्ः
sthira-sukham-asanam.

MEANING: The posture (asana) for Yoga meditation should be steady, stable, and comfortable

Sutra 2.47 | प्रयत्नशैथिल्यानन्तसमापत्तिभ्याम्:
prayatna shaithilya ananta samapattibhyam.

MEANING: The means of perfecting the posture is that of relaxing or loosening of effort, and allowing attention to merge with endlessness, or the infinite.

4. PRANAYAMA (REGULATION OF BREATH)

The fourth limb, *pranayama*, is generally described as breath control or regulation.

To master this regulation, we begin to direct our energy inward to our breath as a means of expanding and extending our energy or life-force (prana = vital energy, ayama = stretch, expansion and extension).

Patanjali encourages that pranayama should only be attempted after the asanas are mastered so that we can more easily direct our energy inward.

Sutra 2.49 | तस्मिन् सति श्वासप्रश्वास्योर्गतिविच्छेदः प्राणायामः
tasmin sati shvasa prashvsayoh gati vichchhedah pranayamah.

MEANING: Once that perfected posture has been achieved, the slowing or braking of the force behind, and of unregulated movement of inhalation and exhalation is called breath control and expansion of prana (pranayama), which leads to the absence of the awareness of both.

5. PRATYAHARA (WITHDRAWAL OF THE SENSES)

With a comfortable and steady posture (asana), as well as with our energy directed inward through pranayama, we can begin the fifth limb, *pratyahara*, or withdrawal of our senses.

This withdrawal allows us to objectively observe our cravings and attachment to senses. As our mind is released from the power of the senses, it turns inward and becomes passive.

Sutra 2.54 | स्वविषयासंप्रयोगे चित्तस्य स्वरूपानुकारैवेन्द्रियाणां प्रत्याहारः

sva vishaya asamprayoge chittasya svarupe anukarah iva indriyanam pratyaharah.

MEANING: When the mental organs of senses and actions (indriyas) cease to be engaged with the corresponding objects in their mental realm, and assimilate or turn back into the mind-field from which they arose, this is called pratyahara.

Sutra 2.55 | ततः परमावश्यता इन्द्रियाणाम्ः

tatah parama vashyata indriyanam.

MEANING: Through that turning inward of the organs of senses and actions (indriyas) also comes a supreme ability, controllability, or mastery over those senses inclining to go outward towards their objects.

6. DHARANA (CONCENTRATION), DHYANA (MEDIATION), AND SAMADHI (FREE ATTENTION)

Patanjali groups the last three limbs under the term samyama - the integration of the body, breath, mind, intellect, and self.

Dharana meaning - The controlled mind that is gained in *pratyahara* (the 5th limb) gives rise to our ability to intensify our attention on a single point.

Sutra 3.1 | देशबन्धः चित्तस्य धारणा:

deshah bandhah chittasya dharana.

MEANING: Concentration (dharana) is the process of holding or fixing the attention of mind onto one object or place, and is the sixth of the eight rungs.

7. DHYANA

When this concentration is prolonged through an uninterrupted flow, it becomes *dhyana*. In dharana, we experience release, expansion quietness and peace, freeing us from attachment. This freedom results in the indifference to the joys of pleasure or the sorrows of pain.

Sutra 3.2 | तत्र प्रत्ययैकतानता ध्यानम्:

tatra pratyaya ekatanata dhyanam.

MEANING: The repeated continuation, or uninterrupted stream of that one point of focus is called absorption in meditation (dhyana), and is the seventh of the eight steps.

8. SAMADHI

The final limb of yoga, samadhi (sama = level or alike, adhi = over or above), is achieved when the object of meditation engulfs the meditator and self-awareness is lost.

In this state the knower, the knowable, and the known become one. This is the final stage on the eightfold path and is ultimate fruit of yoga.

> Sutra 3.3 | तदेवार्थमात्रनिर्भासिं स्वरूपशून्यमिवसमाधिः
> tad eva artha matra nirbhasam svarupa shunyam iva samadhih.

MEANING: When only the essence of that object, place, or point shines forth in the mind, as if devoid even of its own form, that state of deep absorption is called deep concentration or samadhi, which is the eighth rung.

8

THE RELEVANCE OF BHAGWAD GITA IN HINDUISM

A SUMMARY OF THE BHAGAVAD GITA

BY JAYARAM V

The Bhagavad Gita teaches us how to live in this world, do our duties and yet remain like the lotus leaves in the water of life. The world in which we live is said to be a world of illusion. You cannot depend upon it forever, because it is transient and subject to change.

Out of ignorance and egoism, states the Bhagavad Gita, we bind ourselves to it through our desires and desire-ridden actions and suffer from ignorance and delusion, not knowing our true nature and true purpose. Having become caught in the snare of desires and delusion, we remain chained to the cycle of births and deaths and to the forces of nature.

The Bhagavad Gita teaches us how to escape from this predicament, not by escaping from the burdens of the worldly life, nor by the avoidance of our duties and responsibilities, but remaining amidst the humdrum of life and facing it squarely with fearlessness, detachment and stability of mind, accepting God as the Doer and the Savior and performing our actions as part of the sacrifice of life.

According to the Bhagavad Gita, salvation is possible neither for those who want to escape from life and activity nor for those who indulge in sinful, selfish and evil actions and become their own enemies, ignoring their duties and obligations to God. Those who remain amidst the world and its snares, unafraid of the burdens of life, and live their lives with a sense of sacrifice, fully surrendering to God, are truly qualified for it.

The scripture assures that God responds to his devotees with love. Different people approach him with different mindsets and expectations. However, he considers them his dearest devotees, who go through the battles of life with discipline, knowledge and intelligence, do their part in creation and surrender to him with devotion and faith. They are the most qualified to attain liberation and enter the world of Brahman from where there is no return.

Thus, the Bhagavad Gita is about human suffering and its resolution through spiritual effort. It brings spirituality to worldly life and suggests how to face the challenges and compulsions of human life with faith and devotion, without becoming lost in egoistic pursuits and selfish actions. The discourse is about the predicament of humans in the battle of life, with God as its controller.

RELEVANCE OF BHAGAVAD GITA – THE GUIDE TO LEAD OUR LIFE AS PER VEDIC CULTURE IN TODAY'S MODERN WORLD.

The *Bhagavad-Gita* deals essentially with the spiritual foundation of human existence. It is a call of action to meet the obligations and duties of life; yet keeping in view the spiritual nature and grander purpose of the universe. The Bhagavad Gita is one of the first texts in which the importance of religion is discussed with references to the people's everyday life, thus, the role of religion and faith is accentuated with the help of demonstrating the connection with the real-life situations and possible moral choices.

Krishna helps Arjuna to act morally while describing the basic religious principles valued according to the Hindu tradition. Krishna focuses on the importance of improving the person's karma with the help of selfless actions and meditation.

These religious rituals are actively practiced by the representatives of the Hindu culture and tradition because they are the part of their everyday life and vision of the person's progress. From this point, the religious fundamentals described in the Bhagavad Gita are extremely important for the Hindu people, and this fact emphasizes the role of religion within the Hindu society.

In spite of fact that the Bhagavad Gita was written many centuries ago, its role for the Hindu religion & its impact on the accentuation of the role of religion in the society and Hindu culture are significant because the scripture provides the main religious principles which became the fundamentals of the people's everyday life & action.

Thus, the Bhagavad Gita is one of the main sources of the religious and ethical knowledge in the Hindu culture that is why this scripture is often discussed by researchers in the context of the text's role for stating the principles of the Hindu religion and the main ethical norms and ideals connected with the religious visions and in the context of the role of religion in the society because the representatives of the Hindu culture regulate their everyday life with references to the religious norms.

BHAGVAD GITA'S - THE 12 LAWS OF KARMA IN HINDUISM

12 LAWS OF KARMA

THE GREAT LAW	THE LAW OF CREATION
WHATEVER WE PUT INTO THE UNIVERSE WILL COME BACK TO US.	LIFE DOES NOT HAPPEN BY ITSELF, WE NEED TO MAKE IT HAPPEN.
THE LAW OF HUMILITY	THE LAW OF GROWTH
ONE MUST ACCEPT SOMETHING IN ORDER TO CHANGE IT.	WHEN WE CHANGE OURSELVES OUR LIVES CHANGE TOO.
THE LAW OF RESPONSIBILITY	THE LAW OF CONNECTION
WE MUST TAKE RESPONSIBILITY FOR WHAT IS IN OUR LIVES.	THE PAST, PRESENT AND FUTURE ARE ALL CONNECTED.
THE LAW OF FOCUS	THE LAW OF GIVING AND HOSPITALITY
WE CANNOT THINK OF TWO DIFFERENT THINGS AT A SAME TIME.	OUR BEHAVIOR SHOULD MATCH OUR THOUGHTS AND ACTIONS.
THE LAW OF HERE AND NOW	THE LAW OF CHANGE
WE CANNOT BE PRESENT IF WE ARE LOOKING BACKWARD.	HISTORY REPEATS ITSELF UNTIL WE LEARN FROM IT AND CHANGE OUR PATH.
THE LAW OF PATIENCE AND REWARD	THE LAW OF SIGNIFICANCE AND INSPIRATION
THE MOST VALUABLE REWARDS REQUIRE PERSISTENCE.	REWARDS ARE A RESULT OF THE ENERGY AND EFFORT WE PUT INTO IT.

1. *"As you sow, so shall you reap"*, or better known as **"The Great Karma Law"**, means that our thoughts, actions, choices, and decisions have good or bad consequences.

2. *"What we desire comes through participation"*, or better known as **"The Law of Creation"**, means that our intentions determine the evolution of creation and that we have a huge responsibility.

3. *"Refusal to accept what is will still be what is"*, or better known as **"The Law of Humility"**, means that we first need to accept the present circumstances before we can change them.

4. *"Our growth is above any circumstance"*, or better known as **"The Law of Growth"**, means that the only thing that we can control is ourselves.

5. *"Our lives are of our own doing, nothing else"*, or better knowns as **"The Law of responsibility"**, means that if we want to change our life, then we need to modify our mind and our surroundings.

6. *"Everything in the Universe is connected, both large and small"*, or better known as **"Karma's Law of Connection"**, means that everything is connected. Our past, our present, and our future are connected.

7. *"One cannot direct attention beyond a single task"*, or better known as **"The Law of Focus"**, means that we need to direct our full attention to achieve any desired task.

8. *"Demonstrating our selflessness shows true intentions"*, or better known as **"The Law of Hospitality and**

Giving", means that we must manifest into actions all of the things we claim to believe.

9. ***"The Present is all we have"***, or better known as **"The Law of Here and Now"**, means that we shouldn't observe our past choices and grieve over them because we can't change them now.

10. ***"History repeats itself unless changes"***, or better known as **"Karma's Law of Change"**, means that history will continue along the unconstructive road until positive energies change her direction.

11. ***"Nothing of value is created without a patient mindset"***, or better known as **"The Law of Patience and Reward"**, means that rewards do not represent the result and that the real joy and happiness come during the journey, not when the journey is over.

12. ***"The best reward is one that contributes to the whole"***, or better known **as "The Law of Significance and Inspiration"**, means that all the choices should have positive effects on everybody and everything.

These 12 laws of Karma should be practised and it is for us, on own, to make it happen in every phase of our life. If we cannot abide by all of them, all of the time, just using few of these laws of Karma daily, will make our life reach to next level.

BHAGVAD GITA – 18 CHAPTERS – ITS INTERPRETATION & MEANING

BHAGWAD GITA
IN ONE SENTENCE PER CHAPTER...

Chapter 1	Wrong thinking is the only problem in life.
Chapter 2	Right knowledge is the ultimate solution to all our problems
Chapter 3	Selflessness is the only way to progress & prosperity
Chapter 4	Every act can be an act of prayer
Chapter 5	Renounce the ego individually & rejoice in the bliss of infinity
Chapter 6	Connect to the Higher conciousness daily
Chapter 7	Live what you learn
Chapter 8	Never give up on yourself
Chapter 9	Value your blessings
Chapter 10	See divinity all around
Chapter 11	Have enough surrender to see the Truth as it is
Chapter 12	Absorb your mind in the Higher
Chapter 13	Detach from maya & attach to Divine
Chapter 14	Live a lifestyle that matches your vision
Chapter 15	Give priority to Divinity
Chapter 16	Being good is a reward in itself
Chapter 17	Choosing the right over the pleasant is a sign of power
Chapter 18	Let Go, Lets move to union with God

The Bhagavad-Gita consists of 18 chapters. Each chapter is called a Yoga. Yoga is the science of the individual consciousness attaining communion with the Ultimate Consciousness. So, each chapter is a highly specialized Yoga revealing the path of attaining realization of the Ultimate Truth.

The first six chapters have been classified as the **Karma Yoga** section as they mainly deal with the science of the individual consciousness attaining communion with the Ultimate Consciousness through actions. These chapters are:

Chapter 1: **Visada Yoga**	Versus - **47**
Chapter 2: **Sankhya Yoga**	Versus - **72**
Chapter 3: **Karma Yoga**	Versus - **43**
Chapter 4: **Jnana Yoga**	Versus - **42**
Chapter 5: **Karma Vairagya Yoga**	Versus - **29**
Chapter 6: **Abhyasa Yoga**	Versus – **47**

The middle six chapters have been designated as the **Bhakti Yoga** section as they principally are pertaining with the science of the individual consciousness attaining communion with the Ultimate Consciousness by the path of devotion.

Chapter 7: **Paramahamsa Vijnana Yoga**	Versus - **30**
Chapter 8: **Aksara-Parabrahman Yoga**	Versus - **28**
Chapter 9: **Raja-Vidya-Guhya Yoga**	Versus - **34**
Chapter 10: **Vibhuti-Vistara-Yoga**	Versus - **42**
Chapter 11: **Visvarupa-Darsana Yoga**	Versus - **55**
Chapter 12: **Bhakti Yoga**	Versus - **20**

The final six chapters are regarded as the **Jnana Yoga** section as they are primarily concerned with the science of the individual consciousness attaining communion with the Ultimate Consciousness through the intellect.

Chapter 13: **Ksetra-Ksetrajna Vibhaga Yoga**	Versus – **34**
Chapter 14: **Gunatraya-Vibhaga Yoga**	Versus - **27**
Chapter 15: **Purusottama Yoga**	Versus - **20**

Chapter 16: **Daivasura-Sampad-Vibhaga Yoga**   Versus - **24**

Chapter 17: **Sraddhatraya-Vibhaga Yoga**   Versus - **28**

Chapter 18: **Moksa-Opadesa Yoga**   Versus – **78**

TOTAL CHAPTERS - 18   TOTAL VERSUS – 700

SUMMARY

Chapters 1 to 6 = **Karma yoga, the means to the final goal**

Chapters 7 to 12 = **Bhakti yoga or devotion**

Chapters 13 to 18 = **Jnana yoga or knowledge, the goal itself**

9

THE '7' STEP CORRELATION OF BHAGVAD GITA & SAPTAMSIDHI – PATHWAY TO "MOKSHA"

The Bhagavad Gita, contains profound wisdom. It is the most ancient, dissected and discussed scripture of the world. It has 700 verses which are divided into 18 chapters. Each of them is about a Yoga. The following is a summary of the Bhagavad Gita which reflects the salient features of Lord Krishna's teachings.

1. KNOW THAT YOU ARE NOT THE BODY BUT THE SPIRITUAL SELF

The first lesson of the Bhagavad Gita is about knowing who we truly are and what we represent because most of our problems arise from our mistaken notions of who we are. We tend to identify ourselves with our physical personalities since it is the most visible aspect of ours. Thereby, we fail to know our spiritual nature and our deeper connection with God and eternal life. The scripture makes it clear we are not mere physical beings but spiritual entities. Hence, we should not fear death, decay and transience.

The body is the field of activity (Kshetra), in which God or the Self dwells as the Knower of the Field (Kshetrajna). The body is made up of five great elements, the senses, subtle senses, mind, ego and intelligence. It is the seat of desires, attachments, feelings, emotions and such other modifications. The knower of the body is the Supreme Brahman, or the Self, who resides in the body as the indwelling witness and the ultimate enjoyer.

The body is an aspect of Prakriti, which the scripture describes as the city with nine gates. The knower of the body is Purusha, who keeps it alive with his presence. All actions, movements and modifications arise in the field of Prakriti from the Gunas, while the Purusha is the witness, the Guide, and the Non-doer. Seated in Prakriti, he enjoys the objects of Prakriti. Enveloped by the impurities of Nature such as ignorance and delusion, he becomes bound to the mortal world.

The Bhagavad Gita reminds us that the body is unreal because it is a mere outer covering, and temporary. It is like a garment worn by the self. We should not accept our physical identities as our true identities because we are spiritual beings. There is a Self in each of us, which is hidden and transcendental. It is the ultimate reality of our existence and universally present in all living beings as an aspect of the Supreme Self. It is real, permanent, immortal, indestructible and beyond the grasp of the mind and the senses. Hence, it is known only when one transcends them.

2. STABILIZE YOUR MIND BY OVERCOMING DESIRES

Your mind is the seat of your desires, thoughts and feelings. Your wandering senses keep your mind in a state of turmoil. They are responsible for your desire for sense objects and your attachment to them. Your desires and attachments in turn subject you to conflicting emotions and mental instability, as you respond to the pairs of opposites with attraction or aversion according to your inherent nature.

An unstable mind is characterized by egoism, attachments and desire ridden actions. A person of unstable mind is not fit for salvation. His consciousness keeps wandering around sense objects, and he remains entangled in the distractions of the world. The instability of the mind is therefore the first problem, which an aspirant has to resolve to know himself and achieve liberation.

However, how can anyone stabilize his mind? The Bhagavad Gita suggests that only by disengaging the mind from the external world and withdrawing into oneself one can stabilize it. It is not an easy task. Through self-discipline a devotee should restrain his senses and develop detachment from the sense objects. Then only he can experience peace and equanimity. With the attainment of inner tranquillity, his mind becomes stabilized in silence, and his suffering would come to an end. Then, he can easily establish his mind in God and achieve union with him.

3. DO YOUR DUTY WITH DETACHMENT, RENOUNCING THE DOERSHIP

By merely restraining your senses and controlling your mind, you will not be able to free your soul from the cycle of births and deaths. For success on the path, you have to cultivate detachment and remain free from attraction and aversion to things, besides knowing the difference between actions that bind you and actions that free you. You should engage in performing your obligatory duties as a selfless service and an offering to God, renouncing the desire for their outcome. In other words, you must live without expectations, free from desires, without abandoning your duties and obligations.

Not all actions are the same. There are actions, which bind you, and actions, which free you. One should also know the difference between action, inaction and inaction in action and action in inaction. When desires are involved, both actions and inaction become binding, whereas when they are absent action or inaction does not bind. This is the secret to avoid sinful consequences which arise from your actions. It is also why one should avoid performing actions.

The Bhagavad Gita says that none can escape from actions or remain inactive even for a moment. Whoever is born on earth is helplessly driven to action by his inborn gunas (modes or tendencies). Therefore, a devotee should better perform his obligatory duties, with an attitude of renunciation, without seeking to personally benefit from them.

Actions should never be shunned, because the world cannot continue without people performing their duties. Therefore, one should uphold Dharma and undertake God's duties upon earth, knowing that action is superior to inaction and of actions selfless actions are the best because they do not produce karma. The renunciation of doer-ship is also important. While performing actions, one should not think that one is the doer, nor should there be any attachment to them.

An ignorant person acts with attachment, thinking, "I am the doer," whereas the wise person who has overcome delusion and ignorance knows that he is merely doing his duty as an obligation to God. He acts without attachment, for the sake of the world and God. For him there is no interest in what is being done or not to be done, nor does he depend upon anyone for anything. For him all actions become offerings.

This is karma yoga. God exemplifies it through his own actions. Actions do not taint him, even though he engages in them, because he is complete in all respects and has no desire for their outcome. A wise person lives and acts like God. He has the complete knowledge of actions and knows the various methods by which sacrifices are performed. Knowing thus, with the help of such knowledge, he becomes free from the consequences of his actions. His actions become burnt up in the fire of wisdom, and he attains peace as his mind becomes stabilized in the Self.

4. TRUE RENUNCIATION IS RENUNCIATION OF DOERSHIP

The conventional belief is that renunciation means giving up the world. The Bhagavad Gita focuses more upon the attitude of renunciation rather than mere physical act of renunciation. It declares that one should not renounce actions nor one's duties and obligations. It is not even practicable. True renunciation is the renunciation of the desire for the fruit of one's actions.

Renunciation of desires and doer-ship are far more important because they are responsible for our sinful karma and our bondage to the mortal world. All actions arise from God in the domain of Nature due to the activity of the gunas. He is the sacrificer, the sacrifice and the object of sacrifice. He is the doer and the deed. The knower of this truth becomes free by that knowledge. While performing his actions, he knows that he is not the doer, and he does nothing at all. He performs them with his mind fixed on God, offering them to him as a sacrifice, without any attachment. Thereby, he remains untouched by sin, just as a lotus-leaf is untouched by the water in which it grows.

A Karma yogi lives and dies for the sake of God. He engages in actions for his inner purification, not to gain worldly things. In performing them, he merely uses his body, mind, senses and intelligence with indifference, giving up all attachment for their outcome and offering the fruit of his actions to God. Mentally renouncing all actions and practising self-control, he happily lives in his body, neither acting nor making others to act. Offering the fruit of his actions to God, he attains peace through Self-realization and becomes one with God.

The scripture declares that a true sanyasi has no attachment to the sense-objects, nor to his actions. He renounces all thoughts about the world and conquers his lower self (mind and body) by (contemplating upon) his higher self. Becoming established in God, he remains the same to the dualities of life such as heat and cold, pleasure and pain, honour and dishonour. For him a clod of earth or a piece of gold is the same. He is equal minded, neutral and the impartial between friends and foes and between saints and sinners alike.

5. ACKNOWLEDGE THE PRESENCE OF GOD IN YOU AND IN EVERYTHING

The Bhagavad Gita refers to both God and Self as the same or as the aspects of the same reality. God is the creator of all. He is hidden in them as their very selves. The imperishable Self resides in the perishable body as the overlord (Adhidaiva) and inner witness (Sakshi). He is the same in all and pervades all. For liberation one should absorb the mind in the contemplation of God or the Self. When the barriers between the two dissolve, one becomes united with God and attains liberation.

What one thinks at the time of death is equally important. At the time of death if a person's mind is engaged in the contemplation of God, he readily attains liberation. Therefore, one should remember God at all times, with the mind and intellect absorbed in Him so that at the time of death it will be easier for him to remember God. By the constant practice of yoga, a devotee achieves single-minded devotion to God. His mind ceases to think of anything else, as he constantly meditates upon him. By that thought alone he attains supreme peace and liberation.

The scriptures describe God as the ultimate reality. He is the support and source of all, without a second. By becoming established in Prakriti, he manifests the worlds and beings and exists in them as their very essence. The whole universe is permeated and enveloped by him. At the beginning of every cycle of creation, he brings forth the worlds and beings and, in the end withdraws them all. Since he is unattached, indifferent and without desires and attachments, his actions do not bind him, nor produce any karma.

We also learn from the discourse that God is both manifested and unmanifested. Worshipping the latter is difficult because he cannot be known. The manifested God performs many duties for the order and regularity of the worlds. As the lord of creation, he acts as the creator, preserver and protector. If the situation goes out of control, he incarnates upon earth to restore Dharma and destroy evil. When he appears upon earth in physical form, deluded people do not recognize him or acknowledge his greatness, whereas the wise ones who are endowed with discretion, know his true nature and worship him with unwavering devotion.

6. SURRENDER TO GOD WITH DEVOTION

The implied message of the Bhagavad Gita is that all Yogas eventually culminate in devotion to God. Devotion is the highest expression of selfless love, in which devotees seek nothing but the love of God and his constant presence. Although he is impartial and shows no favours, he readily responds to his devotees. They are dearer to him who worship him with single minded devotion, always thinking of him, and forever absorbed in his thoughts. Such people are never lost to him. He takes care of their duties and responsibilities and looks after them.

The scripture gives the subtle hint that one should worship the highest, supreme Brahman rather than the gods and demigods. People may worship God or his numerous form according to their knowledge and wisdom. Those who worship other gods also in a way worship Him only because he is the Lord of all and the final recipient of all offerings. However, those who worship others go to them, but those who worship him attain him only in the end.

God is the epitome of unconditional love. He readily reciprocates the love and devotion of his devotees and accepts whatever offering they make to him with love and devotion. Therefore, the scripture suggests that everything should be offered to God before one enjoys it. In other words, whatever you do, eat, pour into the sacred fire, give as charity or perform as a penance, it should be offered to Him only with pure devotion and without expectations. Lord Krishna states that through pure devotion, by constantly thinking of him and worshipping him, doing actions for his sake, taking refuge in him and renouncing all fruits of actions, controlling the mind and body, with no expectations, steady of mind, a devotee can easily attain God. Such a devotee is very dearer to God, and he takes care of him in every possible way.

7. KNOW THE TRUTH ABOUT THE THREE GUNAS

References to the gunas are found throughout the Bhagavad Gita, except in the first chapter. The Gunas are the basic modes or tendencies, which influence the movement, direction and orientation of all animate and inanimate objects in God's creation. They are universal, permeate all objects and beings and determine their properties and inherent nature. The gunas are different from the tattvas or the finite realities of Nature, but more pervasive. Hence, they influence even the tattvas and their behaviour. The gunas also have the tendency to compete with each other and predominate. They have an impact on our thinking and behaviour. Since they induce desires, the Bhagavad Gita declares that all actions arise from the gunas only.

The gunas are three namely Sattva, Rajas and Tamas. In the primordial Nature, they are in perfect equilibrium but in creation they are present in different permutations and combinations, which is why we have so much diversity in creation. In humans, they are responsible for desires, attachments, desire ridden actions and thereby bondage. By knowing the gunas and their basic propensities, a devotee can overcome their influence and achieve perfection. Through detachment, renunciation, transformative practices, devotion and the grace of God, he can overcome the triple gunas and attain salvation.

The scripture explains the nature of each guna and its influence. Sattva is pure and luminous. It binds the soul to the world through the desire for happiness and knowledge. Rajas is born of passion. It binds the soul through the desire for the fruits of actions. Tamas is born of ignorance and indolence. It is responsible for the grossness of the mind and body. It binds the soul through the desire for rest, inertia, slothfulness and indolence. These three gunas bind the soul to the illusion and chain of births and deaths.

CONCLUSION

The Bhagavad Gita is a practical philosophy. Its teaching can be applied to every aspect of human life. In the teachings of Lord Krishna, you can discern an integrated approach in which you can combine the best of all the Yogas to achieve the four aims of human life, namely Dharma, Artha, Kama and Moksha, without risking your liberation or incurring sinful karma. From the scripture, we learn the importance of leading a divine centered life, in which every action becomes an offering and act of worship.

The solution to the problem of suffering is overcoming desires by practising detachment, renunciation, selfless actions, devotional services, equanimity, sameness and discretion. One should not renounce action, nor avoid doing obligatory duties, but dutifully perform them for the sake of God and offer them to him without expectations. By combining the best of the prescribed Yogas namely karma yoga, jnana yoga, sanyasa yoga, atma samyama yoga and bhakti yoga, casting away egoism and demonic qualities, overcoming the impurities, and cultivating pure devotion, one can escape from the cycle of births and deaths. Actions performed in this manner do not bind people. Always engaged in some action, taking shelter in him, by his grace, they attain the eternal, imperishable Abode.

The Bhagavad Gita is called the secret knowledge. It contains ordinary secrets as well as utmost secrets. In ancient times, it was probably taught to qualified students only. Hence, it is also considered an Upanishad. For this reason, Lord Krishna says that the knowledge of the Bhagavad Gita should never be spoken to anyone who is not austere, who is without devotion, who has no desires, who does not listen and who speaks ill of God. However, whoever teaches it to his devotees with supreme adoration to him, he will attain Him without any doubt.

10

THE RITUALS IN HINDUISM

There are three major schools of thought about the ultimate nature of reality, and virtually all psychological and scientific models of mind can be classified as belonging to one of these three, which are defined as follows:

1. **Theism:** is the belief in the existence of God (a supreme being or spiritual reality), an immortal soul, or any other type of deity or deities.
2. **Atheism:** is the belief in the nonexistence of God (or any type of soul or deity), which in the modern world is often expressed as the materialist hypothesis that matter is the only reality.
3. **Agnosticism**: is the belief that the question of whether or not God (or any type of soul or deity) exists either has not been or cannot be answered

The History of Hindu Rituals: The Aryans, like most religious people throughout the world, considered ritual much more important than doctrine and belief. The Veda itself was a manual of ritual, not of creed statements or theology.

A ritual is a set of actions, performed mainly for their symbolic value. It may be prescribed by a religion or by the traditions of a community. The term usually excludes actions which are arbitrarily chosen by the performers.

The field of ritual studies has seen a number of conflicting definitions of the term.

A ritual may be performed on specific occasions, or at the discretion of individuals or communities.

It may be performed by a single individual, by a group, or by the entire community; in arbitrary places, or in places especially reserved for it; either in public, in private, or before specific people.

A ritual may be restricted to a certain subset of the community, and may enable or underscore the passage between religious or social states.

The Purposes of Rituals: These are varied; with religious obligations or ideals, satisfaction of spiritual or emotional needs of the practitioners, strengthening of social bonds, social and moral education, demonstration of respect or submission, stating one's affiliation, obtaining social acceptance or approval for some event-or, sometimes, just for the pleasure of the ritual itself.

Rituals of various kinds are a feature of almost all known human societies, past or present.

They include not only the various worship rites and sacraments of organized religions and cults, but also the rites of passage of certain societies, atonement and purification rites, oaths of allegiance, dedication ceremonies, coronations and presidential inaugurations, marriages and funerals.

In psychology, the term ritual is sometimes used in a technical sense for a repetitive behaviour systematically used by a person to neutralize or prevent anxiety.

Ritual Actions: There are hardly any limits to the kind of actions that may be incorporated into a ritual.

The rites of past and present societies have typically involved special gestures and words, recitation of fixed texts, performance of special music, songs or dances, processions, manipulation of certain objects, use of special dresses, consumption of special food, drink, or drugs, and much more.

Religious rituals have also included animal sacrifice, human sacrifice, and ritual suicide.

Ritual lamentation-song performed with weeping in many societies was regarded as required to ritually carry the departed soul to a safe place after life.

Many Hindu rites and ceremonies take place in a temple setting and are directed toward a god or goddess, but by no means do all such rituals take place in the temple; indeed, many Hindu rituals are distinctly domestic affairs, taking place in individual homes.

And certainly not all rites and ceremonies are directed toward the gods and goddesses. Virtually every aspect of Hindu life, in fact, is marked by ritual actions.

The different kinds of rituals the Aryans practiced, the purposes for which they were intended and the persons who performed them.

Major Rituals practised by Hindu individuals are mentioned below briefly:

1. **Home Rituals:** Home rituals were probably simple sacrifices at the domestic fires, where the father served as priest by offering food to the devas in the morning and evening. The purpose was to honour the gods and to acknowledge one's dependence on them.

2. **Shamanic Rituals:** A ritual specialist called an Atharvan performs the shamanic rituals. Aryan families call upon this priest to provide help during times of crisis, such as sickness, times of transition, such as birth, naming, initiation; and during auspicious days, such as harvest time.

    The name Shaman is a term used cross-culturally to refer to those persons who have special access to the spiritual world and are able to use that connection for the benefit of others.

    The Atharvan could do more than just heal, provide protection from demons and snakes, promote good luck in gambling, could cause misfortune for one's enemies.

    There are many persons who conduct similar sorts of rituals for healing, providing protection from devils and foretelling the future through astrology and other means.

3. **Religious Rituals:** In religion, a ritual can comprise the prescribed outward forms of performing the cultus, or cult, of a particular observation within a religion or religious denomination.

Although ritual is often used in context with worship performed in a temple, the actual relationship between any religion's doctrine and its ritual(s) can vary considerably from organized religion to non-institutionalized spirituality, a ritual in many cases expresses reverence for a deity or idealized state of humanity.

4. **Rituals Associated with Puja:** It is often translated simply as worship. It literally means honour. This is important, because the practice of and beliefs behind puja involve not just a formal veneration of the gods and goddesses, but also the entering into a particular sort of relationship.

    Puja involves the reception, honouring, and in a sense the entertaining of the deity; in puja, a personal relationship, often a very affectionate relationship, is formed.

    Pujas are performed at a variety of different levels-from the simple pujas performed in the home to elaborate and more formal temple pujas.

    Fundamentally, puja involves bhakti, in that one must approach and treat the god with selfless love; indeed, this is the way in which bhakti is most typically put into practice.

    Significantly, this love is thought to flow both ways: the devotee loves the god, and the god also loves the devotee. Puja (worship), popularly often consisting of singing and sometimes dance, are offered in temples, but many Hindus visit the temple primarily to **"see"** the deity (known as darshan).

5. **Rituals Associated with Bathing in a Sacred River such as the Ganges:** In addition to ancient temples, rivers (such as the Ganges) and places, such as Varanasi, are also sacred. The Ganges (or Ganga as it is known - Indian Journal of Positive Psychology, 2013, 4(1), 87-95 (ISSN 2229-4937 in India) is said to flow from Shiva's matted hair. Nature is herself holy, a reminder that the whole world emanates from the divine.

6. **Rituals Associated with Sculptures and Images of Gods in Home Shrines:** Murtis (images) of the deities are washed, bathed, and treated with great reverence. They are housed in the inner sanctuary of Mandirs, or temples, although most Hindu homes have domestic shrines, where the images are also venerated and treated in the same way. Mandirs are regarded as sacred places.

7. **Rituals Associated with Sacred Places of Pilgrimage:** Varanasi, one of the oldest holy cities in the world. It is considered as one of the most sacred places of pilgrimage for Hindus irrespective of denomination. There are other pilgrimages places like Char Dham in Uttrakhand, Dwarkadhish in Gujarat, Tirupatiji in South India etc.

8. **Rituals Associated with Marriage:** On their marriage day, all Hindus represent the ideal couple, Ram and his consort, Sita. Marriage repays debts to one's ancestors. Bride and groom circle the sacred fire and knot their clothes together as a symbol of unity.

9. **Rituals Associated with Hindu Festivals:** Hindu festivals are popular forms of devotion in which many Hindus participate, regardless of class. Holi is the spring

and harvest festival. People cover each other in paint at this festival, which symbolizes the equality of all people.

Diwali, often called the festival of lights, celebrates among other events, the triumphant homecoming to Ayodhya of the ideal couple, Ram and Sita, after Sita's rescue from the clutches of the evil demon-king, Ravana.

Raksha Bandhan is a ceremony in which brothers, who are symbolically tied to their sister, pledge to protect them.

10. **Rituals Associated with Shraddha:** The ritual of Shraddha not only repays debts towards deceased ancestors, but also makes it easy to repay debts towards God and Sages. Sages are considered to be hot tempered in comparison to God and due to this nature, they could curse one and thus entrap the embodied soul.

However, as debts towards ancestors need to be repaid by actions, it becomes simple and easy to repay these debts through the ritual of Shraddha. Therefore, in order to be able to repay other debts in a good manner, it is necessary that everyone relies upon debts towards ancestors that act as link between God and Sages, satisfy them by performing these rituals and try to embark upon the progress towards attaining final liberation.

By performing the ritual of Shraddha, with the help of the ancestor's souls one can slowly progress towards reaching God and Sages and by the virtue of combined support from Vasu, Rudra and Aditya (Vasu means aspirations, Rudra means dissolution and Aditya means radiance or action), one can provide momentum to the deceased father, grandfather and great grandfather and in turn acquire blessings from God.

11. **Rituals Associated with Sadhana:** Hinduism is practiced through a variety of spiritual exercises, primarily loving devotion (Bhakti Yoga), selfless service (Karma Yoga), knowledge and meditation (Jnana Yoga).

    These are described in the two principal texts of Hindu Yoga: The Bhagavad Gita and the Yoga Sutras.

    The Upanishads are also important as a philosophical foundation for this rational spiritualism.

    The yoga sutras provide a sort of taxonomy of paths (or faiths) that links together various Hindu beliefs and can also be used to categorize non-Hindu beliefs that are seen as paths from margas to moksha, or nirvana.

12. **Rituals Associated with Sacrifices for Special Occasions:** Sacrifice was the primary religious activity of the Vedic period, and although the concept of sacrifice has undergone dramatic transformation as Hinduism has developed over the past few thousand years, it remains the bedrock of the tradition, and Vedic sacrifices continue to be performed throughout the Hindu world.

    Vedic sacrifice is a highly structured affair. Strict rules govern the purifying preparations for the Brahmin priests, construction of the altar, the preparation of the offering-in the contemporary world, various vegetable and grain offerings, particularly ghee (clarified butter) and the performance of the ritual itself. All of this is to satisfy the gods and thereby maintain order, or dharma.

13. **Rituals Associated with Death:** It not only marks the end of life, but also marks the transition to the next life.

The shraddha, funeral rites, therefore, are among the most important rituals in Hinduism. Such rituals are called samskaras, rites of passage.

It is utterly important that the rituals associated with death-not only the cremation itself but also the preparation of the corpse and the purification of the surviving family-be performed properly, because if they are not, the deceased may become stuck between this life and the next, and remain in the world as a preta - a ghost, to haunt the surviving relatives.

Death ritual, traditionally led by the eldest son or nearest male relative, involves the cremation of the deceased on a funeral pyre. Ashes are usually scattered in a sacred river, especially the Ganges.

Additionally, often the family will journey to a tirtha, a crossing of a sacred river, at set points after the death and sink a portion of the deceased cremated remains, further insuring a safe passage to the next life.

I) RITUALS ASSOCIATED WITH VEDIC PUJA (RELIGIOUS RITUAL)

Hindu gods and goddesses are understood to be active forces in the world. Through a variety of rituals, they are made present to their devotees.

Temples are sacred because they are where the gods and goddesses live, and where humans have access to them. Temples are also where many, although by no means all, Hindu rituals are performed.

PRIMARY SYMBOLS IN HINDUISM: There are two primary symbols associated with Hinduism, the AUM and the SWASTIKA. The AUM symbol is composed of three Sanskrit letters and represents three sounds (a, u and m), which when combined are considered a sacred sound. The Aum symbol is often found at family shrines and in Hindu temples. The word Swastika means "good fortune" or "being happy" in Sanskrit, and the symbol represents good luck.

HINDU GODS: Hindus worship many gods and goddesses in addition to Brahman, who is believed to be the supreme God force present in all things.Some of the most prominent deities include:

Brahma	:	the god responsible for the creation of the world and all living things
Vishnu	:	the god that preserves and protects the universe
Shiva	:	the god that destroys the universe in order to recreate it

Devi	:	the goddess that fights to restore dharma
Ganesh	:	the god of luck for all auspicious beginings
Krishna	:	the god of compassion, tenderness and love
Lakshmi	:	the goddess of wealth and purity
Saraswati	:	the goddess of learning

Despite common belief, most Hindus only believe in one Supreme god who is the true nature of reality and the empirical cosmic truth.

According to Hindu texts, God is omnipresent, omniscient, all-knowing, and infinite not bound by the laws of physics. God is found in living and nonliving things, because the universe and all its beings are one.

With this belief, God is present in every person and animal we meet, as well as things like the wind and the sun.

This allows Hindus to select their own personal gods to worship, that act as deities, or a simpler representation of the Supreme god.

There is a main trinity of deities consisting of Brahma (the creator), Vishnu (the preserver or maintainer), and Shiva (the destroyer). There are also several other deities of gods and goddesses that Hindu's worship. Other than these deities, Hindus believe in avatars of deities like Vishnu, who reincarnate into this world whenever it is overcome by evil.

God exists in three forms simultaneously	
Brahman/ Paramatma/ Parabrahma. (Absolute Impersonal Form)	Brahman/Cosmic Spirit. Absolute, Unborn, One without Second, Beyond Time & Space, Ultimate Reality, Infinite, Formless, Without physical body, Invisible, Indivisible, Unmanifest, Truth, Pure Consciousness, Bliss, Peace, Knowledge, Omniscient, Omnipresent, Omnipotent, Immanent, Eternal, Immovable, Immutable, Indestructible, Indescribable, Genderless, Voiceless, Cause of Everything, Self of Brahman is like infinite transcendental Space
Celestial Personal Form	Brahma, Vishnu, Shiva, Goddess Shakti. Divya Kaya is body of pure bliss and clear light emanation of Absolute Spirit.
Avatara (Human form)	Rama, Krishna. Manusyakaya is body which manifests in space and time.
Absolutely seen, only the Brahmakaya is ultimate reality; the Divyakaya and Manusyakaya are "provisional ways of talking about and apprehending it". Brahmakaya is true nature of all Major personal deities. Personal deities are in Oneness with Brahmakaya.	

Existence of God in 3 Different Forms

Every Hindu kid must learn following main mantras by heart:

Gayatri Mantra
ॐ भूर्भुवः स्वः तत् सवितुर्वरेण्यं भर्गो देवस्य धीमहि धियो यो नः प्रचोदयात्...

Shri Ganesh Mantra:
वक्रतुण्ड महाकाय सूर्यकोटि समप्रभ। निर्विघ्नं कुरु मे देव सर्वकार्येषु सर्वदा॥

Mahamrityunjay Mantra
ॐ त्र्यम्बकं यजामहे सुगन्धिं पुष्टिवर्धनम् । उर्वारुकमिव बन्धनान् मृत्योर्मुक्षीय मामृतात् ॥

Shakti Mantra:
या देवी सर्वभूतेषु शक्ति रूपेण संस्थिता। नमस्तस्यै, नमस्तस्यै, नमस्तस्यै नमो नमः॥

Shri hari Vishnu Mantra:
शान्ताकारं भुजग-शयनं पद्मनाभं सुरेशं विश्वाधारं गगन-सदृशं मेघवर्ण शुभाङ्गम्।
लक्ष्मीकान्तं कमल-नयनं योगिभिर्ध्यानगम्यम् वंदे विष्णु भवभय हरं सर्वलोकैक नाथं

Lakshmi Mantra:
ॐ श्री ह्रीं श्रीं कमले कमलालये प्रसीद श्रीं ह्रीं श्रीं ॐ महालक्ष्मयै नमः।

Saraswati Mantra:
या देवी सर्वभूतेषु विध्या रूपेण संस्थिता। नमस्तस्यै, नमस्तस्यै, नमस्तस्यै नमो नमः॥

Shri Ram Mantra:
राम रामेति रामेति, रमे रामे मनोरमे। सहस्रनाम तत्तुल्यं, रामनाम वरानने॥

Shri Krishna Mantra:
मूकं करोति वाचालं पंगु लंघयते गिरिम्। यत्कृपा तमहं वन्दे परमानन्द माधवम्॥

Hanuman Mantra:
ॐ नमो हनुमते भय भंजनाय सुखं कुरु फट् स्वाहा॥

Basic & Important Mantras in Hinduism

THE ABR (ACT, BELIEF & RELEVANCE) CONCEPT OF VEDIC PUJA RITUALS IN HINDUISM:

		1
SR.	ACT	BELIEF
1	**Why do we light a Lamp ?**	Light symbolizes knowledge; and darkness symbolizes ignorance. Knowledge removes ignorance just as light removes darkness. Light being the very important source of life in this universe is worshipped as the supreme natural force i.e. GOD. We light a lamp to bow down with reverence to and acknowledge light and knowledge as the greatest of all forms of being that exists on this planet.
2	**Why do we have a Prayer (Puja) Room / Space ?**	As Lord is all-pervading. To remind us that he resides in our home with us, we have a prayer room. Without the grace of Lord, no task can be successfully or easily accomplished. We invoke his grace by communing with him in the prayer room each day, and on all special occassions.
3	**Why do we blow the Conch ?**	When the conch/bell is blown/rang the primordial sound of AUM emanates. AUM is an auspicious sound that was chanted by the Lord before creating the world. It represents the world and the truth behind it.
	&	
4	**Why do we ring the Bell?**	
5	**Why do we chant AUM?**	The vibration of AUM symbolizes the manifestation of GOD in form. AUM is the reflection of absolute reality; it is said to **anadi-ananta**-without beginning or end - embracing all that exists. AUM symbolises everything - the means & the goals of life, the world & the truth behind it, the material & the sacred, the form & the formless

2	3
RELEVANCE	**EFFECT**
Light is the illuminator of true knowledge and knowledge being the greatest of all forms of wealth supports all our actions whether good or bad. We, therefore keep a lamp lit during all occasions as a witness to our thoughts and actions.	When a lamp filled with pure cow ghee is lit, it attracts divine or positive vibrations from the atmosphere and divinizes the place.
For the purpose of meditation, worship and prayer, we should have conducive atmosphere, hence the need of a prayer room. Spiritual thoughts and vibrations accumulated through regular meditations, worship and chanting done there pervade and influence the minds.	The divine vibrations - created by lighting a cow ghee lamp, grounding sandalwood, burning aromatic incense and offering fresh flowers makes the puja room feel solaced and peacefull. Holy activities and meditation fill this room with good vibrations and full of positive energy.
The auspicious sound of conch / bell is to drown or mask negative comments or noises that may disturb or upset the atmosphere or the mind of the worshippers.	The conch / bell sound elevates people's mind to a prayerfull attitude. Blowing the conch / bell cleanses the nearby surrounding by destroying the harmfull bacteria in the atmosphere and also makes them in-active.
AUM is one of the most chanted sound symbols of India. Most mantras & vaidika prayers start with AUM. All auspicious actions begins with AUM. It is even used for greetings -AUM, HARI AUM & so on. It is repeated as a mantra or meditated upon. Its form is worshipped, contemplated upon or used as an auspicious sign.	AUM creates a highly charged positive aura and elevates the spiritual level and leaves a profound effect on the mind and the body of the chanter as well as on the surroundings. AUM is a unique sound that vibrates into the cosmos and penetrates deep within our psyche, it dispels all inner illusions & melts away negativity.

SR.	ACT	1 BELIEF
6	**Why do we say "SHANTIH" thrice ?**	It is believed that ***"trivaram satyam"*** - that which is said thrice comes true. We chant shanti thrice to emphasise our inner desire for peace. All obstacles problems & sorrows originate from 3 sources ***Adhidaivika***-The unseen divine forces over which we have little or no control like earthquakes, floods & volcanoes. ***Adhibhautika***-The known factors around us like accidents human contacts, pollution and crime. ***Adhyatmika*** - Problems of our bodies and minds like diseases, anger and frustrations.
7	**Why do we do Aarati ?**	Having worshipped the Lord with love by performing abhishek, decorating the image and offering fruits and delicacies, whilst performing the aarati, we see the beauty of the Lord in all his glory. Our mind gets focussed on each limb of the Lord illumined, by the light of the aarati. The singing, clapping, ringing of the bell & so on denote the joy and auspiciousness which accompanies the vision of the Lord.
8	**Why do we worship the Kalasa ?**	A Kalasa is a brass, mud or copper pot filled with water. 9 or 11 mango leaves are placed in the mouth of the pot & a coconut is placed over it. A red or white thread is tied around the neck of the pot & decorated with design. The water in the kalasa symbolises the primordial water from which the entire creation emerged. The leaves and coconut represents creation. The thread represents the love that binds all in creation. Thus the kalasa is considered auspicious and worshipped.

2	3
RELEVANCE	**EFFECT**
"Shantih" means peace, is a natural state of being & where there is peace there is happiness. To invoke peace we chant prayers, by chanting prayers peace is experienced internally. All peace invoking prayers end by chanting Shantih thrice, so that peace will prevail over the three forces that upset the balance in our life and effect our innate peace. Therefore to restore peace, we chant *"Aum Shanti, Shanti, Shanti.....hi"* while concluding a puja, an aarti, havana and all other vedic rituals.	The first utterance of the word is chanted aloud, addressing the unseen forces of nature. The second chant is softer, directed to our immediate surroundings and all those around us. The third chant is the softest, because it is meant for oneself, to address our past life's karmic debts. It is by chanting thus that we strive to regain our lost tranquility.
The aarati of enshrined idols & images when done after all the ritualistic worship - the divine & positive aura expands due to heat and all those who are present receive divine vibrations & gain spiritual strength. The atmosphere of the puja space & temple periphery is charged with enhanced positivity & one receives divine vibrations & blessings of the Creator even without being a part of the ritualistic worship.	Aarti is performed by holding a lighted lamp in the right hand & waving the flame in a clockwise circling movement to light the entire form of the Lord which enhances the intensity in our prayers. At the end of Aarti, we place our palms over the aarti flame, then gently touch our eyes & the top of our head. While doing so, we mentally pray - May the aarti light up our intellect; may our vision be divine & our thoughts be noble & well meaning.
A Kalasa is placed with due rituals on all important occassions like the traditional house warming (griha - pravesa), wedding, navratri festival and daily worship. Symbolically it is placed near the entrance as a sign of welcome and greeting holy personages with a purna kumbha (full pot) acknowledging their greatness and as a sign of respectful and reverential welcome.	The water of the kalasa is sprinkled over the head of the devotees as a blessing and around the house after rituals, to sanctify all. A hand full of unbroken grains of rice when filled in kalash along with water it is called *Purnakalash.* The rice in the pot is termed as *Akshat* or unbroken grains of rice symbolizing eternal blessings on the devotee & his family as well as this akshat has an unique quality of being able to absorb the negativity of the prevailing enviroment.

		1
SR.	**ACT**	**BELIEF**
9	**Why do we offer a Coconut ?**	Coconut is considered as the most auspicious fruit for all vedic rituals and plays a significant role in human beings life throughout. It has the potency to draw divine vibrations from the outer world and which can ward off the ill effects of an evil eye. It is the most common offering in the temple. We offer a coconut at the feet of a deity symbolically signifying we offer our head, implying total surrender to the divine by detaching our ego from the self.
10	**Why do we worship a Tulasi plant?**	Almost every traditional Indian home has an alter bearing a tulasi plant or a potted one in modern homes. The lady of the house lights a lamp, waters the plant, worships and circumambulates it. It is one of the most sacred plant used in the ritualistic worship, which once used can be washed & reused again - as it is considered self-purifying. Tulasi leaf is always placed on the food offered to the Lord.
11	**Why do we offer Jal (water) to Surya (sun)?**	The Lord Surya is considered as the soul of the universe. according to Hindu Mythology. The Lord Surya gives knowledge, divinity and performance. According to Hindu astrology, Sun is the significator of the soul. That is why the Hindu people in India do offer water to sun. The Lord Surya is the lord of all the planets on the heavenly body and the most powerfull one. The Sun God gives power, position, authority, glory, name, reputation, force and makes one a ruler or a kingly person.

2	3
RELEVANCE	**EFFECT**
Tender coconut water is used in abhishek rituals (purification & cleansing act), since it is believed to bestow spiritual growth on the seeker. The white kernel of broken coconut is later distributed to devotees as **Prasadam.** Due to its deemed sacredness, it is offered while undertaking a new venture, inaugration ceremonies, building a house, dam etc. buying a new vehicle or entering a new house, celebrating festivals, during weddings and so on.	Coconut is offered to please the Lord or to fulfill our desires & its water is sprinkled to remove negativity of an effected area & also to purifiy place. The shape of the fruit is akin to a human head with three eyes. When it is offered to a diety, it should be offered with the eye side facing the diety as this is the sensitive side of the fruit that can receive divine vibes from the idol. It is broken, symbolising the breaking of the human ego.
Tulasi leaves are an essential ingredients of the **"Panchamrita"** in a puja ceremony. In Vaishnava philosphy, Tulasi leaves please Lord Vishnu the most. Rosaries-tulsi malas are made from the dried stems of the plant and use it while reciting Visnu mantras. Apart from relegious significance tulasi leaf has great medicinal value & is used to cure various ailments. It is a rich antioxidant.	Necklaces made of small tulsi beads are own by the pious. It develops a magnetic field around a person and also checks dissipation of his static energy. Tulasi leaves can obsorb ultra-voilet radition, which is why tulasi leaves are placed on food items during an esclipse-to protect them from radition. Organic Tulasi has been developed for the first time as a stress reliever and energizer.
Sun has a miraculous effect on our health, wealth, knowledge, power and position etc. If we stand in front of the Tulsi and pour the water, it supplies abundant fresh oxygen and it will benefit oneself in deep pure breathing. When the ray of sunlight passes through, the stream of water which flows down the kalash or vessel it reaches our eye & helps in powering eyesight. Offering Jal to surya regularly elevates one spiritually. The best time to offer water to the sun God is between 6 AM to 7 AM.	Sun Rays are pure white in color and while we offer water to the sun we see the rays through the flowing water. The spectrum of rays passing through water gets refracted and breaks into seven colors. This dispersed light now enters our body & balances the seven colors (Chakras) in our body. Morning sun rays are very powerful sun rays and are a source of vitamin D. When we stand in rays of sun our chest absorbs the maximum sunlight. After we take bath our body pores are open and we can absorb energy from the sun positively.

SR.	ACT	1 BELIEF
12	**Why do we fast (Upavasa) ?**	Fasting in sanskrit is called ***"Upavasa"*** - 'Upa' means near & 'vasa' means to stay, coined together means 'Staying near the Lord' - meaning the attainment of close proximity with the Lord. Fasting gives it a spiritual connotation of dieting for a higher cause - as a vow to please the Lord or to fullfill ones desires & to develop will power, control the senses or as a form of austerity.
13	**Why do we do Pradikshina - Circumambulate a Diety in a Temple) ?**	When we visit a temple, after offering prayers, we circumambulate the temple/ deity with folded hands often chanting prayers. This is called ***"Pradikshina"***. It is done in clockwise direction. The Supreme Lord is the source, centre & the essence of our lives. Recognising him as the focal point of our lives, we go about doing our daily chores.
14	**Why do we wear marks (Tilak) on the forehead ?**	The Tilak invokes a feeling of sanctity in the wearer & others. It is recognised as a relegious mark. Its form and colour vary according to one's caste, relegious sect or the form of the Lord worshipped. The Chandana, Kumkum & Bhasma which is offered to the Lord is taken back as prasada and applied on our foreheads.

2	3
RELEVANCE	**EFFECT**
Fasting is a self-imposed form of discipline (tapas), it is usually adhered to Joy. Abstaining oneself from eating from a relegious context, makes the mind pure & alert, and its a self control promise which strengthens our will & confidence. The Bhagaavad Gita urges us to eat neither too less or too much, i.e. ***"Yukta Aahar"***, even while not fasting.	As the body machine and its system needs a break & an overhaul to work at its best. Rest & change of diet during fasting are very good for the digestive system and the entire body. It cultivates control over senses, sublimate our desires and guide our minds to be poised and at peace.
When we circumambulate, we remind ourselves to lead an auspicious life of righteousness, with the Lord who is the indispensable source of strenghth & help. We thereby overcome our wrong tendencies and avoid repeating the wrong doings of the past.	When we circumambulate, we receive divine forces because the idol constantly emanates energy in all directions and we receive that exalted power from all the directions and thus rejuvenate ourselves to face the challenges of life.
When applying the Tilak, one prays, 'I remember the Almighty; may pious feelings pervade in all my activities; may I be right righteous in my deeds. The tilak covers the spot between the eyebrows, which is a seat of memory & thinking. It is known as the Ajna Chakra.	The Tilak seeks the Almighty's blessings and serves as a guard against negative forces. The entire body emanates energy in the form of electromagnetic waves, specially the forehead area. The chandana, bhasma & kumkum cools the forehead by protecting us and prevents energy loss.

II) RITUALS ASSOCIATED WITH SPECIAL OCCASIONS (MAJOR FESTIVALS)

A) MAHASHIVRATRI: THE NIGHT OF SHIVA

The most sacred festival of Shiva falls on the 14th night of the new moon, during the dark half of the lunar month of Phalguna. This is some time between February and March. This is Mahashivratri or the great night of Shiva.

Devotees of Shiva stay awake the entire night on this auspicious night of Shivratri. Some perform poojas, chant Vedic mantras or Rudram, practice sadhana and meditation. These sacred practices bestow a sense of peace within us and oneness with the world.

"Every Mahashivratri is meant to wake up every particle of your body. The festival is a wake-up call to move away from conflicts and move towards truth, beauty, peace, and benevolence - the ethereal qualities of Shiva." - Gurudev Sri Sri Ravi Shankar.

This night brings a sense of deep serenity and benevolence. ***Any meditation done on this day is a hundred times more effective.***

It is also astrologically linked: when the sun and moon are in a particular alignment, it helps to elevate the mind. Ancient seers said such days were congenial for spiritual practices. According to Indian astrology, there are certain days and time frames in a year that are conducive to spiritual growth and meditation. Mahashivratri is one such day. In the daily hustle and bustle of life, we forget our source of energy - that which is running us. *Mahashivratri* is a festival to remember and to take our awareness to the basis of our existence: ***Shiva.***

MAHASHIVARATRI STORY SURROUNDING THIS OCCASION:

- One is that Lord Shiva married Parvati on this day. So, it is a celebration of this sacred union.

- Another is that when the Gods and demons churned the ocean together to obtain ambrosia that lay in its depths, a pot of poison emerged. Lord Shiva consumed this poison, saving both the Gods and mankind. The poison lodged in the Lord's throat, turning him blue. To honor the savior of the world, Shivratri is celebrated.

- One more legend is that as Goddess Ganga descended from heaven in full force, Lord Shiva caught her in his matted locks, and released her on to Earth as several streams. This prevented destruction on Earth. As a tribute to Him, the Shivalinga is bathed on this auspicious night.

- Also, it is believed that the formless God Sadashiv appeared in the form of a Lingodhbhav Moorthi at midnight. Hence, people stay awake all night, offering prayers to the God.

Mahashivratri is the day to honour and celebrate Lord *Shiva*—honour life and celebrate existence. Most people spend the day of *Mahashivratri* in prayer, meditation and celebration.

ACCORDING TO THE SHIVA PURANA, THE MAHASHIVARATRI PUJA INVOLVES:

Performing Shiva Puja, the worship of Lord Shiva, is a sacred and revered practice in Hinduism.

1. **Purification (Achamana):** Begin by purifying yourself by washing your hands, feet, and face. Sip a few drops of

water while chanting "Om Keshavaya Namaha" or any other mantra.

2. **Preparation of the Altar:** Set up an altar or sacred space for the puja. Place a Shiva Lingam or an image of Lord Shiva at the center of the altar. Decorate it with flowers, incense, and lamps.

3. **Offerings (Asana and Arghya):** Offer a seat (asana) to Lord Shiva and perform arghya by offering water with a conch or your right hand while chanting "Om Namah Shivaya."

4. **Bathing the Shiva Lingam (Abhishekam):** Perform the Abhishekam by pouring water, milk, honey, ghee, and other sacred liquids over the Shiva Lingam. Chant the "Rudra Sukta" or other Shiva mantras during the Abhishekam.

5. **Dressing the Shiva Lingam:** After the Abhishekam, dress the Shiva Lingam with clean and fresh clothes or symbollically with a pure white cotton, normally used for making the cotton wick for preparing the oil and ghee lamp. Offer sandalwood paste, kumkum (vermilion), and turmeric to the Lingam.

6. **Offer Bilva leaves :** Offer Bilva (Bael) leaves on Shiva Lingam, while chanting his names or the "Aum Namah Shivaya" mantra and then offer fresh flowers (preferably white in colour) on Shiva Lingam.

7. **Incense and Lamp Offering (Dhupa and Deepa):** Light incense sticks and wave them in front of the Shiva Lingam. Offer a lamp with ghee or oil dipped in a cotton wick while chanting prayers.

8. **Food Offering (Naivedyam):** Offer fruits, sweets, or any vegetarian dishes as Naivedyam to Lord Shiva. Chant his names or the "Aum Namah Shivaya" mantra.

9. **Water Offering (Achamana):** Offer water to Lord Shiva for drinking.

10. **Arati:** Perform Arati by waving a camphor flame or ghee lamp in front of Lord Shiva while singing the "Om Jai Shiv Omkara" or any other Arati song.

11. **Prayers and Meditation:** Offer your prayers to Lord Shiva and meditate on his divine form. Chant his mantras or sit silently in his presence.

12. **Distribution of Prasad:** Finally, distribute the Prasad (blessed offerings) to all those present during the puja.

Worshipers also apply three horizontal lines of holy ash on their forehead just like the Lord Shiva which represents spiritual knowledge, cleanliness and penance.

They wear garland made up of the Rudraksha (seed of Rudraksha tree) while worshiping the Lord Shiva.

It is essential to perform the puja with a pure heart, devotion, and sincerity. You can chant specific Shiva mantras like "Om Namah Shivaya," "Maha Mrityunjaya Mantra," or the "Shiva Gayatri Mantra" during the puja. The timings and elaborate procedures of Shiva Puja may vary based on individual customs, traditions, and personal preferences.

Lord Shiva Mantras:

- **Shiva Moola Mantra** - *Aum Namah Shivaya*
- **Maha Mrityunjaya Mantra** - *Aum Tryambakam Yajamahe Sugandhim Pushti-Vardhanam, Urvarukamiva Bandhanan Mrityormukshiya Mamritat*

- **Rudra/Shiva Gayatri Mantra** - *Aum Tatpurushaya Vidmahe, Mahadevaya Dhimahi, Tanno Rudrah Prachodayat*

Here is a list of what to do on Mahashivratri:

1. **Observe fasting on the day of Mahashivratri**:
   Fasting detoxifies the body and curtails the restlessness of the mind. A mind that is not restless slips into meditation easily. Therefore, fasting on *Mahashivratri* serves to detoxify the body and aid meditation. It is recommended to fast with fruits or foods that are easily digestible.

2. **Meditate on Mahashivratri**:
   The position of the constellations on the night of *Mahashivratri* is considered very auspicious for meditation. So, it is advisable for people to keep awake and meditate on *Shivaratri*.

   In ancient times, people used to say, 'If you cannot meditate every day, do so for at least one day in a year - on *Shivratri* day - keep awake and do meditation'.

   - **Mahashivratri is the day specially to wake the Divinity that is deep within you**.

3. **Chant *'Aum Namah Shivaya'***
   - *'Aum Namah Shivaya'* is the perfect mantra to chant on *Mahashivratri*, as it immediately elevates your energy.
   - **'Aum'**, in the mantra, refers to the sound of the universe. It means peace and love. The five letters, 'Na', 'Ma', 'Shi', 'Va', 'Ya' in ***'Namah Shivaya'*** indicate the five elements - Earth, Water, Fire, Air, and Ether.

- Chanting 'Aum Namah Shivaya' harmonizes the five elements of the universe. When there is peace, love and harmony in all the five elements, then there is bliss and joy.
- Along with Aum Namah Shivay Chanting you can chant - Shiv Tandav Stotram and Kaal Bhairav Ashtakam – (Specific Vedic Mantras of Lord Shiva).

4. **Attend Mahashivratri Puja or Rudra Puja:**
   Rudra Puja or Mahashivratri Puja is a special ceremony performed to honor Lord Shiva. It involves singing special Vedic mantras accompanied by certain rituals. Rudra Puja brings positivity and purity to the environment and transforms negative emotions. Participating in the Puja and listening to the chants helps the mind slip into meditation effortlessly.

5. **Worship the Shivalinga:**
   Shivalinga is a symbolic representation of the formless Shiva. Worshipping the Shivalinga includes offering **'Bel Patra'** (leaves of the bel tree) to it. Offering *'Bel Patra'* represents offering three aspects of your being - ***Rajas*** (the aspect of you that is responsible for activity), ***Tamas*** (the aspect of you that brings inertia) and ***Sattva*** (the aspect of you that brings positivity, peace, and creativity). These three aspects affect your mind and actions. Surrendering the three to the Divine brings peace and freedom.

LORD SHIVA'S AARTI – AUM JAI SHIV AUMKARA : IN ENGLISH LYRICS.

Aum Jai Shiv Aumkara, Swami Jai Shiv Aumkara।
Brahma Vishnu Sadashiv, Ardhangi Dhara॥
Aum Jai Shiv…
Ekanan Chaturanan Panchanan Raje।
Hansasan Garudasan Vrishvahan Saje॥
Aum Jai Shiv…
Do Bhuj Chaar Chaturbhuj Dashbhuj Ati Sohe।
Trigun Roop Nirakhate Tribhuvan Jan Mohe॥
Aum Jai Shiv…
Akshmala Vanmala Mundmala Dhari।
Chandan Mrigmudh Sohe Bhaale Shasidhari॥
Aum Jai Shiv…
Shvetambar Pitambar Baghambar Ange।
Sankadik Garunadik Bhootadik Sange॥
Aum Jai Shiv…
Kar Ke Madhya Kamandalu Chakra Trishuldharta।
Jagkarta, Jagbharta Jagsanghaar Karta॥
Aum Jai Shiv…
Brahma Vishnu Sadashiv Janat Aviveka।
Pranavakshar Ke Madhye Yeh Teeno Eka॥
Aum Jai Shiv…
Kashi Mein Vishwanath Viraje Nandi Brahmachari।
Nit Uth Darshan Paavae, Mahima Ati Bhaari॥
Aum Jai Shiv…

TrigunswamiJi Ki Aarti, Jo Koi Nar Gaave।
Kahat Shivanand Swami, Manvanchit Phal Paave॥
Aum Jai Shiv…
Aum Jai Shiv Aumkara, Swami Jai Shiv Aumkara।
Brahma Vishnu Sadashiv, Ardhangi Dhara॥
Aum Jai Shiv Aumkara…….॥॥

LORD SHIVA'S AARTI – AUM JAI SHIV AUMKARA : IN HINDI LYRICS.

ॐ जय शिव ओमकारा, स्वामी जय शिव ओंकारा।

ब्रह्मा विष्णु सदा शिव अर्द्धांगी धारा ॥

ॐ जय शिव…॥

एकानन चतुरानन पंचानन राजे ।

हंसानन गरुड़ासन वृषवाहन साजे ॥

ॐ जय शिव…॥

दो भुज चार चतुर्भुज दस भुज अति सोहे।

त्रिगुण रूपनिरखता त्रिभुवन जन मोहे ॥

ॐ जय शिव…॥

अक्षमाला बनमाला रुण्डमाला धारी ।

चंदन मृगमद सोहै भाले शशिधारी ॥

ॐ जय शिव…

श्वेताम्बर पीताम्बर बाघम्बर अंगे ।

सनकादिक गरुणादिक भूतादिक संगे ॥

ॐ जय शिव…॥

कर के मध्य कमंडलु चक्र त्रिशूल धर्ता ।

जगकर्ता जगभर्ता जगसंहारकर्ता ॥

ॐ जय शिव…॥

ब्रह्मा विष्णु सदाशिव जानत अविवेका ।

प्रणवाक्षर मध्ये ये तीनों एका ॥

ॐ जय शिव...॥

काशी में विश्वनाथ विराजत नन्दी ब्रह्मचारी ।

नित उठि दर्शन पावे महिमा अति भारी ॥

ॐ जय शिव...॥

त्रिगुण शिवजीकी आरती जो कोई नर गावे ।

कहत शिवानन्द स्वामी मनवांछित फल पावे ॥

ॐ जय शिव...॥.

ॐ जय शिव ओमकारा, स्वामी जय शिव ओंकारा।

ब्रह्मा विष्णु सदा शिव अर्द्धांगी धारा ॥

ॐ जय शिव ओमकारा.......॥।

B) NAVARATRI: THE NIGHT OF SHAKTI – DEVI. THE "9" DAYS FESTIVAL CELEBRATION OF GODDESS DURGA.

SIGNIFICANCE OF NAVRATRI

In India, Navratri is celebrated with zeal and enthusiasm. It occurs in the month of Ashvin-(Sept-Oct) as per Hindu Calendar. The idol of Maa Durga is worshipped for nine days straight in different forms and on the tenth day, it is immersed in water.

People wish for a good life, healthy mind and body, and pray for spiritual, emotional and physical well-being. The puja rituals are observed for nine days straight, with each day signifying the importance of one avatar or incarnation of Goddess Durga.

The power of devotion is wonderfully drawn forth to adore the divine shakti in all its prowess during these 9 days of Navratri.

The first 3 days are spent worshipping **Goddess Durga** to introspect and defeat the vices and impurities within.

The 4th, 5th and 6th day commemorate **Goddess Lakshmi** who bestows spiritual wealth and prosperity for all times to come.

The 7th, 8th and the 9th day are devoted to worship **Goddess Saraswati**, Goddess of Wisdom to achieve all round success in life with humility.

According to Devi Bhagvat Puran, during the battle of Ramayana, on the eighth day of the waning moon of Ashwin month, Lord Brahma awakened the sleeping mother goddess herself, Durga. Durga explained how to worship her during the Navratri for nine days, and that was exactly carried out by Lord Rama during the Mahanavratri. He killed Ravana on the tenth day, on Vijaya Dashmi or Dussehra.

The story from Markandey Puran is the one you are most likely to have heard. It is about the demon king Mahishasura, who after worshipping Brahma, was blessed with immortality. Soon, he started harassing the innocent, and the Gods asked help from Shiva. The Trinity of Brahma, Vishnu and Shiva created a female warrior, **Adishakti Durga** to defeat Mahisasura. Mesmerised by her beauty, the demon king approached her for marriage. The Goddess accepted it, but with one condition that Mahisasura has to defeat her in the battle. The ever-proud Mahisasura agreed, and the battle lasted for nine nights (hence Navratri). At the end of the ninth night, Adishakti Durga beheaded Mahisasura, and from there comes the name 'Mahisasur Mardini'.

Navratri celebrates these victories of good over evil, and how the **'Shakti'** was able to defeat a proud demon when the Gods of all three Lokas were terrified by the latter.

The nine days are dedicated to different incarnations of Goddess Durga. People follow the custom of wearing the respective colors symbolizing the deity of the day. Here described is the importance of each day and the goddess associated:

NOTE: The below details are as per the Calendar Year-2023, Navratri Festival.

(Each day of Navratri is associated with a specific color, symbolising different forms of Goddess Durga every year. It depends on the day when Navratri starts)

Day 1: Shailputri: Goddess Shailputri: An incarnation of Maa Parvati, is worshipped on this day. In this form, she can be seen sitting on Nandi-the bull with a Trishul in her right hand and Lotus flower in her left one. Color of the day remains Red, which represents courage, vigor and action.

Day 2: Goddess Brahmacharini: On second day of Navratri, Goddess Brahmacharini is worshipped. She is said to be one of the many incarnations of Maa Parvati who became Sati, the pure one. One worships the Goddess to attain moksha or salvation and peace. Color of the day remains Blue, which depicts calmness and positive energy. In this form, she can be seen holding a kamandalu and japmala in her hands while walking bare-feet.

Day 3: Goddess Chandraghanta: This Mata is worshipped on the third day of Navratri. The name was derived after Maa

Parvati got married to Lord Shiva and adorned a half-moon on her forehead. Yellow, the color of the day, depicts bravery.

Day 4: Goddess Kushmanda: This goddess is worshipped on the fourth day of Navratri. She can be seen sitting on a Lion with eight hands. She is said to be the one endowing vegetation and greenery on Earth, which is why color of the day remains Green.

Day 5: Goddess Skandmata: She is the mother of Lord Kartikeya or Skanda, Goddess Skandamata, is revered on the fifth day. She can be seen having four arms, holding her small baby and riding a fierce lion. She depicts the mutating power of a mother when she realizes her child is in danger. Color of the day remains Grey.

Day 6: Goddess Katyayani: A violent incarnation of Goddess Durga and daughter to Sage Katya, Goddess Katyayani is worshipped on the sixth day. She represents courage and is seen having four hands and riding a lion. Color of the day remains Orange.

Day 7: Goddess Kalratri: Maa Kalratri is known to be the ferocious form of Goddess Durga and worshipped on Saptami. Color of the day remains White. It is believed that Maa Parvati's fair skin got transformed into black in order to kill Sumbha and Nisumbha, two demons.

Day 8: Goddess Mahagauri: Mahagauri Mata is worshipped on the eighth day of Navratri, and symbolizes peace and intellect. Color of the day remains Pink, which represents positivity.

Day 9: Goddess Siddhidatri: The ninth day is known to be Navami, and **Maa Siddhidatri**, also called as Ardhanareeswara, is worshipped. She is said to possess all kinds of Siddhis. She can be seen sitting on a Lotus and has four hands. Devotees wear Purple to symbolize her Divine Aura.

MANTRAS TO BE RECITED DURING NAVRATRI

Mantras Dedicated To Goddess Durga For The First Three Nights Of Navratri

> Om Dum Durgayaia Namaha
> ॐ दम दुर्गायय नमः ॥

Mantras Dedicated To Goddess Lakshmi For The Second Three Nights Of Navratri

> Om hrim Mahalakshmyai Namaha
> ॐ ह्रीम महालक्ष्म्यै नमः ॥

Mantras Dedicated To Goddess Saraswati For The Last Three Nights Of Navratri

> Om Aim Saraswatyai Namaha
> ॐ ऐं सरस्वत्यै नमः ॥

NAVRATRI PUJA VIDHI

- Wake up early in the morning, take a bath and wear clean clothes.
- Arrange a thali for puja with all puja ingredients in it.
- Place the idol or picture of Goddess Durga on a red-coloured cloth.
- Place the claypot, sow the barley seeds and sprinkle some water everyday till Navami.

- In an auspicious muhurat, carry out the process of urn installation or Ghatasthapana. Fill the urn with Gangajal, and place mango leaves on the top of its mouth. Wrap the neck of the urn with sacred red thread or Moli, and coconut with red chunri. Place the coconut on the top of mango leaves. Place the urn near or on the claypot.

- Carry out panchopchar puja of the deities, which includes worshipping with flowers, camphor, incense sticks, scent and cooked dishes.

- Chant Maa Durga Mantras throughout these nine days and ask for prosperity. Invite her into your house and ask her to grace your house with her presence.

- On the eighth and ninth day, carry out the same puja and invite nine girls at your house. These nine girls represent nine forms of Goddess Durga. Hence, wash their feet, offer them a clean and comfortable seat. Worship them, apply tilak on their forehead and serve them delicious food.

- On the last day of the Durga puja, carry out Ghata Visarjan. Say your prayers, offer flowers and rice to the deities and remove the Ghata from the altar, and then after perform the Visarjan (immersing the idol in river or a flowing water stream and bid farewell accompanied with prayer and reverence to Maa Durga.

माँ दुर्गा आरती - *MAA DURGA AARTI LYRICS IN HINDI*

जय अम्बे गौरी, मैया जय श्यामा गौरी।

तुमको निशदिन ध्यावत, हरि ब्रह्मा शिवरी।।

जय अम्बे गौरी,...।

मांग सिंदूर बिराजत, टीको मृगमद को।
उज्ज्वल से दोउ नैना, चंद्रबदन नीको।।
जय अम्बे गौरी,...।
कनक समान कलेवर, रक्ताम्बर राजै।
रक्तपुष्प गल माला, कंठन पर साजै।।
जय अम्बे गौरी,...।
केहरि वाहन राजत, खड्ग खप्परधारी।
सुर-नर मुनिजन सेवत, तिनके दुःखहारी।।
जय अम्बे गौरी,...।
कानन कुण्डल शोभित, नासाग्रे मोती।
कोटिक चंद्र दिवाकर, राजत समज्योति।।
जय अम्बे गौरी,...।
शुम्भ निशुम्भ बिडारे, महिषासुर घाती।
धूम्र विलोचन नैना, निशिदिन मदमाती।।
जय अम्बे गौरी,...।
चण्ड-मुण्ड संहारे, शौणित बीज हरे।
मधु कैटभ दोउ मारे, सुर भयहीन करे।।
जय अम्बे गौरी,...।
ब्रह्माणी, रुद्राणी, तुम कमला रानी।
आगम निगम बखानी, तुम शिव पटरानी।।
जय अम्बे गौरी,...।
चौंसठ योगिनि मंगल गावैं, नृत्य करत भैरू।
बाजत ताल मृदंगा, अरू बाजत डमरू।।
जय अम्बे गौरी,...।
तुम ही जग की माता, तुम ही हो भरता।
भक्तन की दुःख हरता, सुख सम्पत्ति करता।।
जय अम्बे गौरी,...।
भुजा चार अति शोभित, खड्ग खप्परधारी।
मनवांछित फल पावत, सेवत नर नारी।।
जय अम्बे गौरी,...।

कंचन थाल विराजत, अगर कपूर बाती।
श्री मालकेतु में राजत, कोटि रतन ज्योति।।
जय अम्बे गौरी,....।
श्री अम्बेजी की आरती जो कोई नर गावै।
कहत शिवानंद स्वामी, सुख-सम्पत्ति पावै।।
जय अम्बे गौरी, मैया जय श्यामा गौरी।

MAA DURGA AARTI LYRICS IN ENGLISH

Jai ambe gauri, mayya jai shyama gauri,
Tumko nish-din dhyavat, hari brahma shivri,
Jai ambe gauri…
Maang sindoor virajat, tiko mrig-mad ko,
Ujjwal se dou naina, chandra vadan niko,
Jai ambe gauri…
Kanak samaan kalewar, raktaambar raaje,
Rakt pushp gal-mala, kanthan par saaje,
Jai ambe gauri…
Kehri vahan rajat, kharag khapar dhaari,
Sur nar muni jan sevat, tinke dukh haari,
Jai ambe gauri…
Kanan kundal shobhit, naas-agre moti,
Kotik chandra divakar, sum rajat jyoti,
Jai ambe gauri…
Shumbh ni-shumbh vidare, mahisha sur ghati,
Dhumra-vilochan naina, nish-din- mad mati,
Jai ambe gauri…
Chandh mundh sangh-haare, shonit beej hare,
Madhu kaitabh doumaare, sur bhaiheen kare,
Jai ambe gauri…

Brahmani rudrani, tum kamla rani,
Aagam nigam bakhani, tum shiv patrani,
Jai ambe gauri…
Chou-sath yogini mangal gavat, nritya karat bhairon,
Baajat taal mridanga, aur baajat damaroo,
Jai ambe gauri…
Tum ho jag ki maata, tum hi ho bharta,
Bhakto ki dukh harata, sukh sampati karata,
Jai ambe gauri…
Bhuja chaar ati shobit, var mudra dhaari,
Man vaanchit phal pavat, sevat nar naari,
Jai ambe gauri…
Kanchan thaal virajat, agar kapoor baati,
Shri maal-ketu me rajat, kotik ratan jyoti,
Jai ambe gauri…
Shri ambe-ji-ki aaarti, jo koi nar gave,
Kahat shivanand swami, sukh sampati pave,
Jai ambe gauri, mayya jai shyama gauri.

C) GANESHOTSAVA: GANESH CHATURTHI – THE "11" DAYS FESTIVAL CELEBRATION OF LORD GANESHA. [(1+10) - INCLUDING FIRST DAY OF INSTALLATION OF DEITY AND 10 DAYS OF PUJA & CELEBRATION]

In Indian culture, Ganesha is considered as the giver of education and wisdom; destructor of hurdles; benedictory; provider of security, Siddhi, prosperity, power, and honour. Though Vinayaki Chaturthi and Sankashti Chaturthi are celebrated every month during bright and dark fortnight respectively, yet this yearly **Vinayaka Chaturthi** is considered most auspicious because Ganesha had appeared on this day. If this **Ganesh Chaturthi** falls on Tuesday, it is considered as **Angarak Chaturthi**, which helps the worshipper in getting rid of all the sins and curses. If this **Sankatahara Chaturthi** falls on Sunday, it is also considered quite auspicious.

In Maharashtra – (state in India) this festival is celebrated as the **GANESHOTSAVA** (Ganesh Festival), which runs till 10 days and ends on **Anant Chaturdashi** (**Ganpati Visarjan**). During these days, Ganesha is beautifully adorned and worshipped. On the last day, Ganesha is immersed in the water with a great pomp and show.

Ganesh Chaturthi is one of the most eagerly awaited festivals in a year celebrated by the Hindus. Ganesh Chaturthi is a 10-day festival that marks the birth of Ganesha, the elephant-headed god. Ganesha, the deity of wisdom and prosperity, is the son of Lord Shiva and Mother Parvati. This festival is celebrated with great fanfare, joy, and good food.

Ganesh Chaturthi is celebrated every year in the Bhadrapada (Aug/Sept) month's fourth day of bright fortnight. As per the beliefs, Lord Ganesha was born on this day during Madhyahan Kaal on Monday in Swati Nakshatra and Leo ascendant. That's why this one is considered as the main Ganesh Chaturthi or **Vinayaka Chaturthi**.

GANESH CHATURTHI VRAT & PUJA VIDHI

1. The one who is observing fast must take the idol of Ganesha made of gold, copper, mud, etc. after getting over with the daily morning rituals.

2. After filling a new Kalash with water, cover its mouth with a new cloth and place Lord Ganesha over it.

3. After offering vermillion and durva, bring 21 Laddoos as the holy food. Keeping 5 Laddoos for Ganesh Ji, offer rest of them to the Brahmins and needy people.

4. Ganesha must be worshipped in the evening. After reciting Ganesh Chaturthi Katha, Chalisa, and Aarti, offer water to the Moon without looking at it.

5. On this day, Siddhi Vinayak incarnation of Ganesha is worshipped.

Note:

a. Make sure that the basil leaves are not used in the Ganesh Puja. Ganesha likes all leaves and flowers except Tulsi (basil).

b. There is a ritual of circumambulating Ganesha once. Some people believe in doing it thrice.

STEP BY STEP GANESH CHATURTHI PUJA PROCEDURE:

The whole family works as a team to welcome Lord Ganesh Before the arrival of Ganesh Chaturthi, clean the house and make sure your home is neat and organized. On the day of Ganesh Chaturthi, wake up early in the morning and take a holy bath. Ganesh Chaturthi is a happy and sacred occasion. All the members in the family must share the responsibilities and perform the puja together and seek his blessings.

Getting the Ganesh idol

There are three approaches to planning the puja for Lord Ganesh. Some people use the image, picture, or an idol that they already have in their puja room. Alternatively, you can make an idol yourself with the family members using clay or turmeric. New images or idol (murti) of Ganesh can be bought from the shops and pandals. This is the most popular option used by most households. Every year, people go searching for a new idol that they use for prayers and procedures during this ten-day festival.

Setting up the altar for Lord Ganesh

Make the seating arrangements for Lord Ganesh on a raised platform or the traditional puja altar of the home. Draw rangoli in front of the altar. Spread a nice-looking cloth on the pedestal or platform. Place the image/idol of Ganesh at the puja altar.

Ganesh Puja

Light a lamp with gingelly oil or coconut oil. Light incense sticks and gather in front of the altar with the family members.

One can give a holy bath to the idol (if the material of the idol is suitable to permit the water). You can do so using rose water, sandal paste, coconut water, honey, panchamrit, and other materials. Wipe the idol with a clean cloth after the holy bath. Decorate the image of Ganesh with sandal paste, vermilion, clothing, ornaments, flowers, and garlands. Chant the mantras of Ganesh and offer flowers at the base of the image/idol.

GANESH SLOKAS & MANTRAS

- *Om Gam Ganapataye Namah!*
- *Vakra Tunda Mahakaya, Surya Koti Samaprabha, Nirvighnam Kurume Deva, Sarva Karyeshu Sarvada.*

- ***Aum Gajaananam Bhuta Ganaadi Sevitam, Kapitta Jambuu Phala Saar Pakshitam,***
Umasutam Shoka Vinaasha Kaaranam, Namami Vighneshwara Paada Pankajam.
- *Shuklambharadharam Vishnum Shashi Varnam Chaturbhujam,*
Prasanna Vadanam Dhyayet Sarva Vighnopa Shantaye.

BASIC GANESHA MANTRA

1. Vakratunda Ganesha Mantra

श्री वक्रतुण्ड महाकाय सूर्य कोटी समप्रभा
निर्विघ्नं कुरु मे देव सर्व-कार्येशु सर्वदा॥

Shree Vakratunda Mahakaya Suryakoti
Samaprabha
Nirvighnam Kuru Me Deva Sarva-Kaaryeshu
Sarvada॥

2. Ganesha Shubh Labh Mantra

ॐ श्रीम गम सौभाग्य गणपतये
वर्वर्द सर्वजन्म में वषमान्य नमः॥

Om Shreem Gam Saubhagya Ganpataye
Varvarda Sarvajanma Mein Vashamanya
Namah॥

3. Ganesha Gayatri Mantra

ॐ एकदन्ताय विद्धमहे, वक्रतुण्डाय धीमहि,
तन्नो दन्ति प्रचोदयात्॥

Om Ekadantaya Viddhamahe, Vakratundaya
Dhimahi,
Tanno Danti Prachodayat॥

Conclusion of the Ganesh Chaturthi puja

Offer prasad and other dishes like modak and ladoos prepared at home for the puja. Offer coconut, fruits and other eatables you have specially brought for Ganesha. Burn camphor at the altar and recite mantras, sing Ganesha songs and perform Aarti all together. Seek the blessings of Lord Ganesha. Distribute the prasad among the family members and invitees.

Note: Continue the puja in the morning and evening till you choose to keep the idol in worship following Ganesh Chaturthi. On the day of Visarjan, you can perform the final puja and bid farewell to Lord Ganesh, seeking his return to your home the next year.

POPULAR - GANESHA AARTI - ENGLISH

JAI GANESH, JAI GANESH, JAI GANESH DEVA
MATA JAKII PARVATII, PITAA MAHAADEVA

EKA DANTA DAYAVANTA, CHAR BHUJA DHAARII
MATHE SINDUURA SOHAI, MUUSE KII SAVARI
JAI GANESH...

ANDHANA KO AANKHA DETA KORHINA
KO KAAYAA
BANJHANA KO PUTRA DETA NIRDHANA
KO MAAYA
JAI GANESH...

HAAR CHARHE, PHOOL CHARHE AURA
CHARHE MEVA

LADDUAN KO BHOGA LAGE SANT KAREN SEVA
JAI GANESHA...

DINAN KI LAAJ RAKHO SHAMBHU PUTRA VAARI
MANORATH KO PURA KARO JAI BALIHAARI
JAI GANESHA...

MUMBAI – TRADITIONAL GANESHA AARTI

SUKHKARTA DUKHHARTA VARTA VIGHNACHI ||
NURVI PURVI PREM KRUPA JAYACHI ||
SARVANGI SUNDAR UTI SHENDURACHI ||
KANTI JHALKE MAL MUKATAPHALAANCHI..||
JAIDEV JAIDEV JAI MANGAL MURTI ||

DARSHAN MAATRE MAN: KAAMNA PHURTI ||
RATNAKHACHIT PHARA TUJH GAURIKUMRA ||
CHANDANAACHI UTI KUMKUMKESHARA ||
HIREJADIT MUKUT SHOBHATO BARA ||
RUNJHUNATI NUPURE(2) CHARANI GHAGRIYA ||
JAIDEV JAIDEV JAI MANGAL MURTI ||

LAMBODAR PITAAMBAR PHANIVARVANDANA ||
SARAL SOND VAKRATUNDA TRINAYANA ||
DAS RAMACHA VAT PAHE SADANA ||
SANKATI PAVAVE NIRVANI RAKSHAVE
SURVARVANDANA ||
JAIDEV JAIDEV JAI MANGAL MURTI ||

DARSHAN MAATRE MAN: KAAMNA PHURTI ||

श्री गणेशजी की आरती

जय गणेश जय गणेश जय गणेश देवा ।
माता जाकी पार्वती पिता महादेवा ।। जय.
एक दन्त दयावन्त चार भुजा धारी ।
माथे सिन्दूर सोहे मूसे की सवारी ।। जय.
अन्धन को आँख देत कोढ़िन को काया ।
बाँझत को पुत्र देत निर्धन को माया ।। जय.
हार चढ़े फूल चढ़े और चढ़े मेवा ।
लड्डुअन का भोग लगे सन्त करे सेवा ।। जय.
दीनन की लाज राखो, शम्भु पुत्र वारी ।
मनोरथ को पूरा करो, जय बलिहारी ।। जय.

Ganesha Aarti in Hindi

श्री गणपतीची आरती
सुखकर्ता दु:खहर्ता

सुखकर्ता दु:खहर्ता वार्ता विघ्नाची ।
नुरवी पुरवी प्रेम कृपा जायची ।
सर्वांग सुंदर उटी शेंदुराची ।
कंठी झळके माळ मुक्ताफळाची ।
जयदेव जयदेव जय मंगलमूर्ती ।
दर्शनमात्रे मन:कामना पुरती जय देव जय देव ।। धृ ।।
रत्नखचित फार तुज गौरीकुमरा ।
चान्दांची उटी कुंकुमकेशरा ।
हिरेजडीत मुगुट शोभती बरा ।
रुणझुणती नुपुरे चरणी घागरिया ।। जय ।। २ ।।
लंबोदर पितांबर फणीवरबंधना ।
सरळ तोंड वक्रतुंड त्रिनयना ।
दास रामाचा वाट पाहे सदना ।
संकटी पावावे निर्वाणी रक्षावे सुरवरवंदना ।
जयदेव जयदेव जय मंगलमुर्ती ।
दर्शनमात्रे मन:कामना पुरती ।। ३ ।।

Ganesha Aarti in Marathi

III) RITUALS ASSOCIATED WITH STAGES OF LIFE - (THE SAMSKARAS)

MAJOR SAMSKARAS IN HINDUISM

Hindu scriptures have prescribed rituals and ceremonies to mark 16 defined stages of life. These 16 cradle-to-cremation rituals are known as **Samskaras.**

They begin with conception and continue with rituals performed before the baby is born.

After the birth, the childhood rituals continue, marking the naming of the child, the first feeding, the first haircut, and the piercing of the ears.

The childhood rituals are followed by ceremonies that initiate the young into adulthood, followed by house-holder related rituals that include the wedding.

The final stages of life bring rituals that prepare the individual for retirement, followed by the rituals to bury or cremate the dead.

These rituals are believed to mark significant life events and purify the mind and soul. Each Samskara has its own significance and is performed according to the guidelines mentioned in the Vedas and other ancient scriptures. The 16 Vedic Samskaras are as follows:

1. **Garbhadhana:** The act of conception, this ceremony is performed by the couple before conceiving a child. It is intended to seek blessings for a healthy and virtuous child.

2. **Pumsavana:** This Samskara is performed during the second or third month of pregnancy. It involves rituals and prayers for the well-being of the mother and the child.

3. **Simantonnayana:** This Samskara is performed during the seventh or eighth month of pregnancy. It involves rituals to ensure a safe and successful delivery.

4. **Jatakarma:** This is the ritual performed immediately after a child's birth to welcome the newborn into the family and the world. It is believed to cleanse the child of impurities and bless them with a prosperous life.

5. **Namakarana:** This Samskara is the naming ceremony performed on the 11th day or 12th day after birth. The child's name is chosen, and prayers are offered for the child's well-being.

6. **Nishkramana:** This Samskara marks the child's first outing, usually when they are taken outside the home for the first time.

7. **Annaprashana:** This is the first feeding ceremony, where the child is introduced to solid food, typically rice or other grains, around six months of age.

8. **Chudakarana:** Also known as Mundan or Tonsure, this Samskara involves shaving off the child's hair, usually in their first or third year. It symbolizes the removal of impurities and negative traits.

9. **Karnavedha:** This Samskara is the ear-piercing ceremony, performed during the first or third year for girls and the third or fifth year for boys.

10. **Upanayana:** Also known as the Sacred Thread ceremony, this Samskara marks the initiation of a child into formal education and spiritual learning. It is typically performed for boys between the ages of 8 and 16.

11. **Vedarambha:** This Samskara involves the beginning of the study of the Vedas after the Upanayana ceremony.

12. **Samavartana:** This is the graduation or completion ceremony for students after completing their formal education, typically around the age of 24.

13. **Vivaha:** This is the wedding ceremony, where the couple solemnizes their union and takes vows for a lifelong commitment to each other.

14. **Vanaprastha:** This Samskara marks the retirement stage of life, where a person gradually withdraws from household responsibilities and focuses on spiritual pursuits.

15. **Sannyasa:** This Samskara involves renunciation, where an individual takes vows to live a life of asceticism and devotion to spiritual pursuits.

16. **Antyeshti:** This is the funeral or last rites ceremony performed after a person's death. It involves the cremation or burial of the deceased and various rituals to guide their soul to the afterlife.

The 16 Vedic Samskaras are considered essential in Hindu tradition as they shape an individual's life journey and mark important transitions from one stage of life to another. Each Samskara is a celebration of life's milestones and an opportunity for spiritual growth and well-being.

IV) RITUALS ASSOCIATED WITH MARRIAGE – (THE MID-LIFE CEREMONY)

VEDIC MARRIAGE – RITUALS & ITS SIGNIFICANCE:

Hinduism has traditionally held that there are certain times and days that are better to hold or to begin important events, such as marriage, particular religious rituals and even business ventures. The times and days of all major religious events are determined by careful consultation of the calendars by priests.

On a more mundane level, many Hindus will consult a priest or other religious figure to determine the proper day for a marriage for each person. There are more and less auspicious times, based on the day and time of their birth, the movements of the planets and stars, and a number of other factors.

Many Hindus have their own astrological charts, made by their parents, shortly after the birth of the child and they will consult and get interpreted it by priests throughout their lives on any special occasions and ceremonies, specially for Marriage purpose.

There is no single standard Hindu marriage ceremony. Regional variation is prevalent in the sequence of rituals comprising the ceremony. There is also considerable flexibility within each ritual. Variation reflects family traditions, local traditions, resources of the families and other factors. Three key rituals predominate, as follows.

a. *Kanyadaan* - In Vedic marriage ceremonies, Kanyadaan is a significant and sacred ritual that holds deep spiritual and cultural significance. Kanyadaan is the act of giving away the bride by her parents or guardians to the groom during the wedding ceremony. The term "Kanyadaan" is derived from Sanskrit, where "Kanya" means "daughter" or "young girl," and "Dan" means "to give."

The essence of Kanyadaan lies in the belief that the bride is considered a precious gift or divine blessing to her parents. By performing Kanyadaan, the parents or guardians symbolically hand over the responsibility of their daughter's well-being, happiness, and future to the groom. It is a moment of emotional and spiritual significance, representing the acceptance of a new family member and the beginning of a new phase in the bride's life.

b.   *Panigrahana* - This is an essential ritual in Vedic marriages, representing the acceptance of the bride by the groom as his life partner. The word "Panigrahan" is derived from Sanskrit, where "Pani" means "hand," and "Grahan" means "to hold" or "to accept." During this ceremony, the groom holds the bride's hand as a symbolic gesture of accepting her as his wife and companion for life.

The Panigrahana ritual holds deep spiritual and cultural significance in Vedic marriages.

c.   *Saptapadi* - Saptapadi, also known as the Seven Steps or Seven Vows, is a significant ritual in Vedic marriage ceremonies. It is one of the most sacred and pivotal aspects of the wedding, symbolizing the seven promises or vows taken by the bride and groom as they walk seven steps together around the sacred fire (Agni). The term "Saptapadi" is derived from Sanskrit, where "Sapta" means "seven," and "Padi" means "steps", and each step corresponding to a pair of vows for groom to the bride, and bride to groom. It holds a deep spiritual and cultural significance in Hindu weddings.

The vows are pronounced in Sanskrit; sometimes also in the language of the couple. Saptapadi is performed in presence of fire, and in many weddings, after each of their seven oaths to each other, the groom and bride perform the ritual of ***Agnipradakshinam*** - walking around the fire, with hands linked or with the ends of their garments tied together.

Fire is the divine witness (to the marriage) and after Saptapadi the couple are considered husband and wife.

KANYADAAN - IN VEDIC CONTEXT

The Kanyadaan ceremony is performed by the bride's father. If the father has died, a guardian of the bride's choosing performs the ritual. The father brings the daughter, then takes the bride's hand and places her hand in the groom's hand.

This marks the beginning of the ceremony of giving away the bride. The groom accepts the bride's hand, while the *kamasukta* (hymn to love) is pronounced, in the presence of the father, the bride and the groom.

THE KAMASUKTA VERSE IS:

Who offered this maiden? to whom is she offered?
Kama (the god of love) gave her to me, that I may love her
Love is the giver, love is the acceptor
Enter thou, the bride, the ocean of love

With love then, I receive thee
May she remain thine, thine own, O God of love
Verily, thou art, prosperity itself
May the heaven bestow thee, may the earth receive thee

After this ritual recital, the father asks the groom to not fail the bride in his pursuit of *dharma* (moral and lawful life), *artha* (wealth) and *kama* (love).

The groom promises to the bride's father that he shall never fail her in his pursuit of *dharma*, *artha* and *kama*. The groom repeats the promise three times.

This repeated promise by the groom marks the end of the *kanyadaan* ritual in the Hindu wedding.

PANIGRAHANA - IN VEDIC CONTEXT

The ritual of *Panigrahana* comes after *Kanyadaan*. It is sometimes preceded by the *vivaha-homa* rite, wherein a symbolic fire is lit by the groom to mark the start of a new household.

Panigrahana is the act of 'holding the hand' ritual, as a symbol of the bride and groom's impending marital union, with the groom acknowledging a responsibility to four deities: *Bhaga* signifying wealth, *Aryama* signifying heavens/milky way, *Savita* signifying radiance/new beginning, and *Purandhi* signifying wisdom.

The groom faces west, and while the bride sits in front of him, with her face to the east, he holds her hand while the following Rigvedic mantra is recited:

I take thy hand in mine, yearning for happiness
I ask thee, to live with me, as thy husband
Till both of us, with age, grow old

Know this, as I declare, that the Gods
Bhaga, Aryama, Savita and Purandhi,
have bestowed thy person, upon me
that I may fulfil, my Dharmas of the householder, with thee

This I am, That art thou
The Saman I, the Rc thou
{Rc – A stanza of a prayer or hymn of Rigveda}
The Heavens I, the Earth thou

This step is also called **Hast-Milap** (literally, "meeting of hands"). The whole ceremony was timed around an auspicious time (*Mauhurat*) for this step and a few decades ago the wedding invitation would even list the time when this event was going to take place.

The Symbolic Act of Sindoor Arpan. Hasta Milap. The Mark of Together-ness

SAPTAPADI (SHORT FORM) - IN VEDIC CONTEXT

The *Saptapadi* (In Sanskrit "seven steps"/"seven feet"; sometimes called **Saat Phere**: "seven rounds") is the most important ritual of Vedic Hindu weddings, and represents the legal element of the Hindu marriage ceremony.

The couple conduct seven circuits of the Holy Fire (*Agni*), which is considered a witness to the vows they make to each other. In some regions, a piece of clothing or sashes worn by the bride and groom are tied together for this ritual. Elsewhere, the groom holds the bride's right hand in his own right hand.

Each circuit of the consecrated fire is led by either the bride or the groom, varying by community and region. Usually, the bride leads the groom in the first circuit.

In North India, the first six circuits are led by the bride, and the final one by the groom.

In Central India, the bride leads the first three or four circuits. With each circuit, the couple makes a specific vow to establish some aspect of a happy relationship and household for each other.

In some South Indian weddings, after each saying a mantra at each of the seven steps, the couple say these words together:

> *"Now let us make a vow together. We shall share love, share the same food, share our strengths, share the same tastes. We shall be of one mind; we shall observe the vows together. I shall be the Samaveda, you the Rigveda, I shall be the Upper World, you the Earth; I shall be the Sukhilam, you the Holder – together we shall live and beget children, and other riches; come thou, O beautiful maiden*

In North Indian weddings, the bride and the groom say the following words after completing the seven steps:

We have taken the Seven Steps. You have become mine forever. Yes, we have become partners. I have become yours. Hereafter, I cannot live without you. Do not live without me. Let us share the joys. We are word and meaning, united. You are thought and I am sound. May the night be honey-sweet for us. May the morning be honey-sweet for us. May the earth be honey-sweet for us. May the heavens be honey-sweet for us. May the plants be honey-sweet for us. May the sun be all honey for us. May the cows yield us honey-sweet milk. As the heavens are stable, as the earth is stable, as the mountains are stable, as the whole universe is stable, so may our union be permanently settled.

THE SAPTAPADI – SAATH PHERE: BOUNDING OF NEW RELATIONSHIP - BY SEVEN STEPS FOR LIVING TOGETHER – A SERIES OF VOWS, THE GROOM & THE BRIDE ARE MADE TO TAKE EACH-OTHER IN HINDUISM CULTURE.

SAPTAPADI (LONG FORM) - DETAILED VERSION IN VEDIC CONTEXT

The long form of *Saptapadi* starts with a preface announced by the priest, introducing a series of vows the groom and bride make to each other, as follows. With the completion of the seventh step the two become husband & wife.

PRIEST'S PREFACE

The world of men and women, united in the bond of marriage by Saptapadi, to further promote the joy of life, together listen with triumph.

STEP 1

Groom's vow: *Oh!, you who feeds life-sustaining food, nourish my visitors, friends, parents and offspring's with food and drinks. Oh! beautiful lady, I, as a form of Vishnu, take this first step with you for food.*

Bride's vow: *Yes, whatever food you earn with hard work, I will safeguard it, prepare it to nourish you. I promise to respect your wishes, and nourish your friends and family as well.*

STEP 2

Groom's vow: *Oh!, thoughtful and beautiful lady, with a well-managed home, with purity of behaviour and thought, you will enable us to be strong, energetic and happy. Oh! beautiful lady, I, as Vishnu, take this second step with you for the strength of body, character and being.*

Bride's vow: *Yes, I will manage the home according to my ability and reason. Together, I promise, to keep a home that is healthy, strength and energy giving.*

STEP 3

Groom's vow: *Oh!, skillful and beautiful lady, I promise to devote myself to earning a livelihood by fair means, to discuss, and let you manage and preserve our wealth. Oh! dear lady, I, as Vishnu form, cover this third step with you to thus prosper in our wealth.*

Bride's vow: *Yes, I join you in managing our income and expenses. I promise to seek your consent, as I manage our wealth, fairly earned, so it grows and sustains our family.*

STEP 4

Groom's vow: *Oh!, dear lady, I promise to trust your decisions about the household and your choices; I promise to dedicate myself to help our community prosper, the matters outside the house. This shall bring us respect. Oh! my lady, I, as Vishnu, take this fourth step with you to participate in our world.*

Bride's vow: *Yes, I promise to strive to make the best home for us, anticipate and provide necessary things for your worldly life, and for the happiness of our family.*

STEP 5

Groom's vow: *Oh!, lady of skill and pure thoughts, I promise to consult with you and engage you in the keep of our cows, our agriculture and our source of income; I promise to contribute to our country. It shall win us future. Oh! my skilled lady, I, as*

Vishnu form, take this fifth step with you to together grow our farms and cattle.

Bride's vow: *Yes, I promise to participate and protect the cattle, our agriculture and business. They are a source of yoghurt, milk, ghee, and income, all useful for our family, necessary for our happiness.*

STEP 6

Groom's vow: *Oh!, lovely lady, I seek you and only you, to love, to have children, to raise a family, to experience all the seasons of life. Oh! my lovely lady, I, as Vishnu, take this sixth step with you to experience every season of life.*

Bride's vow: *Feeling one with you, with your consent, I will be the means of your enjoyment of all the senses. Through life's seasons, I will cherish you in my heart. I will worship you and seek to complete you.*

STEP 7

Groom's vow: *Oh friends!, allow us to cover the seventh step together, this promise, our Saptapad-friendship. Please be my constant wife.*

Bride's vow: *Yes, today, I gained you, I secured the highest kind of friendship with you. I will remember the vows we just took and adore you forever sincerely with all my heart.*

V) RITUALS ASSOCIATED WITH DEATH – ANTYESHTI VIDIHI

ANTYESHTI: DEFINATION

Antyeṣṭi (अन्त्येष्टि) is a composite Sanskrit word of *antya* and *iṣṭi*, which respectively mean "last" and "sacrifice". Together, the word means the **"last sacrifice".** Similarly, the phrase Antima Sanskara literally means "last sacred ceremony, or last rite of passage"

Antyeshti: (Sanskrit: अन्त्येष्टि) - literally means "last sacrifice", and refers to the funeral rites for the dead in Hinduism, which usually involve cremation of the body.

This rite of passage is the last Samskara in a series of traditional life cycle Samskaras that start from conception in Hindu tradition. It is also referred to as Antima Sanskar, Antya-kriya, Anvarohanyya, or as Vahni Sanskara

ANTHESTI: THE HINDUS SCRIPTURAL DEFINATION & REFERENCE

The Antyeshti rite of passage is structured around the premise in ancient literature of Hinduism that the microcosm of all living beings is a reflection of a macrocosm of the universe.

The soul (Atman, Brahman) is the essence and immortal that is released at the Antyeshti ritual, but both the body and the universe are vehicles and transitory in various schools of Hinduism.

The human body and the universe consist of five elements in Hindu texts – air, water, fire, earth and space. The last rite of passage returns the body to the five elements and its origins.

ANTYESHTI: THE HINDUS TRADITIONAL PRACTICE: (IN-BRIEF)

The last rites are usually completed within a day of death.

While practices vary among sects, generally, his or her body is washed, wrapped in white cloth, if the dead is a man or a widow. In red cloth, if it is a woman whose husband is still alive.

The big toes are tied together with a string and a *Tilak* (red, yellow or white mark) is placed on the forehead.

The dead adult's body is carried to the cremation ground near a river or water, by family and friends, and placed on a dry wood pyre with feet facing south.

The eldest son, or a male mourner, or a priest – called the lead cremator or lead mourner – then bathes himself before leading the cremation ceremony.

He circumambulates the dry wood pyre - the body, says a eulogy or recites a hymn, places sesame seeds or rice in the dead person's mouth, sprinkles the body and the pyre with ghee (clarified butter), then draws three lines signifying - *Yama* (deity of the dead), *Kala* (time i.e. deity of cremation) and the dead.

Prior to lighting the pyre, an earthen pot is filled with water, and the lead mourner circles the body with it, before lobbing the pot over his shoulder so it breaks near the head.

Once the pyre is ablaze, the lead mourner and the closest relatives may circumambulate the burning pyre one or more times. The ceremony is concluded by the lead cremator, during the ritual, is *kapala kriya*, or the ritual of piercing the burning skull with a stave (bamboo fire poker) to make a hole or break it, in order to release the spirit.

All those who attend the cremation are exposed to the dead body or cremation smoke, mandatorily take a bath as soon as possible after the cremation, as the cremation ritual is considered unclean and polluting.

The cold collected ash from the cremation is later consecrated to the nearest river or sea.

In some regions, the male relatives of the deceased shave their head and invite all friends and relatives, on the tenth or twelfth day, to eat a simple meal together in remembrance of the deceased. This day, in some communities, also marks a day when the poor and needy are offered food in memory of the dead.

Burial In Hinduism: Apart from the cremation method there are large sects in Hinduism which follow burial of the dead.

The preparatory rituals are more or less similar to cremation viz, washing the body, applying vibuthi or chandan on the forehead of the deceased etc, but instead of cremating, the deceased is buried.

The body is either placed in sleeping position or in some Shaivite and tribal traditions, the body is positioned in sitting position - legs folded and arms resting on the thigh simulating meditative position.

The burial pit is prepared in the community burial ground called **'Shamshana'**, usually situated outside the city or village. Some affluent will bury their dead in their own field.

The burial pit for sleeping position is generally three feet width and six feet in length – (3'x 6') and for sitting position it is three feet by three feet – (3' x 3').

As a thumb rule in all the sects invariable the saints are buried in sitting position in a separate place where later on a Samadhi is built which becomes a place of worship.

Cremation ground: The cremation ground is called *Shmashana* (in Sanskrit), and traditionally it is located near a river, if not on the river bank itself.

Those who can afford it, may - go to special sacred places like **Kashi** (Varanasi), **Haridwar**, **Prayagraj** (Allahabad), **Sri Rangam**, **Brahmaputra** and **Rameswaram** to complete this rite of immersion of ashes into water.

ANTYESHTI: THE HINDUS MODERN PRACTICE: (IN-DETAIL)

Both manual bamboo wood pyres and electric cremation are used for Hindu cremations. For the latter, the body is kept on a bamboo frame on rails near the door of the electric chamber. After cremation, the mourner will collect the ashes and consecrate it to a water body, such as a river or sea.

An overall at A GLANCE, flow diagram of the entire rituals - DEATH RITUAL (ANTYESHTI SANSKARA) in Hinduism.

AT A GLANCE - COMPLETE PROCEDURAL RITES : HINDUISM – DEATH RITUAL (ANTHESTI SANSKAR) :

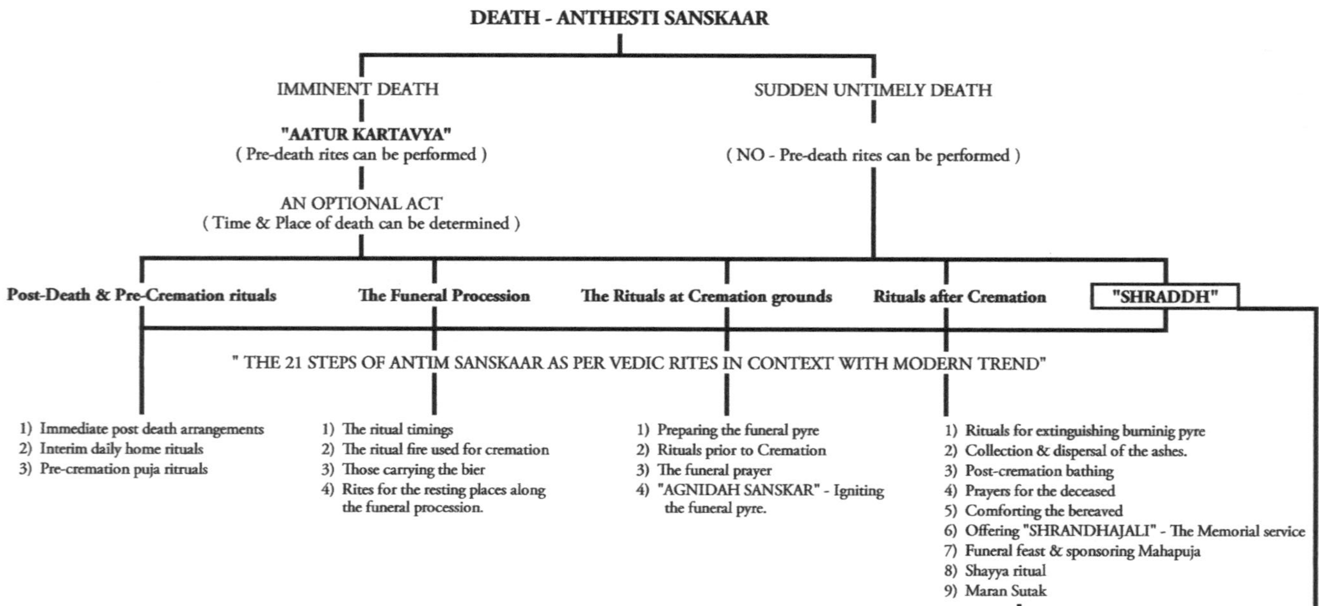

A N T Y E S H T I - THE FINAL PATH TO LIBERATION (MOKSHA)

THE 21 STEPS OF "ANTYESHTI" - ANTIM SANSKAAR – THE LAST JOURNEY - AS PER VEDIC RITES - DESCRIBED IN "7" PROCEDURAL RITUALS FROM THE TIME OF DEATH TILL POST CREMATION ACTIVITIES FOLLOWED BY "SHRADDHA".

1. **AATUR KARTAVYA: Duties before death**
2. **SIGNIFICANCE OF TIME & PLACE OF DEATH –** (Optional / Obsolete in modern practices)
3. **POST DEATH & PRE-CREMATION RITUALS: (3 Steps)**
    a. Immediate post death arrangements
    b. Interim daily home rituals
    c. Pre-cremation puja rituals

4. **THE FUNERAL PROCESSION: (4 Steps)**
   a. The ritual timings
   b. The ritual fire used for cremation
   c. Those carrying the Bier
   d. Rites for the resting places along with the funeral process

5. **THE RITUALS AT CREMATION GROUND: (4 Steps)**
   a. Preparing the funeral pyre
   b. Various rituals just prior to cremation
   c. The funeral prayer
   d. "AGNIDAH SANSKAAR" – Igniting the funeral pyre

6. **RITUALS AFTER CREMATION: (9 Steps)**
   a. Rituals for extinguishing the burning pyre
   b. Collection & dispersal of the ashes
   c. Post-cremation bathing
   d. Prayers for the deceased
   e. Comforting the bereaved
   f. The Memorial Service – "SHRANDDHANJALI"
   g. Funeral feast & sponsoring Mahapuja
   h. Shayya Ritual
   i. Maran Sutak

7. **"SHRADDHA"**

1) AATUR KARTAVYA: DUTIES BEFORE DEATH

a. Devotional songs, chanting of mantras – (Aumkaar dhuvani, Bhagavad Gita path chapter 2nd & 13th, Gayatri Mantra, Guru mantra), Religious discourse or a very light soft music should be played-on.

b. On doctor's indication if death is close or if the sufferer is slipping into unconsciousness, immediately should seek-out for his/her last wishes and attempt to bring them on fruition.

c. When the Atma (Soul) is leaving its physical body & the person is on the brink of death, the person should be laid on the ground with the head to the North direction (As north facing eases the movement of the Atma)

d. If the son is present, the dying person's head should be placed on the son's lap & a lamp should be lit, so that the dying person can see it.

e. A leaf of Tulsi plant & a holy water (Ganga water) or any sanctified water should be placed in the dying person's mouth.

f. Offerings (in-form of charity/donation) should be made to the sadhus & the needy.

2) SIGNIFICANCE OF TIME & PLACE OF DEATH:

According to the modern belief any time and all places of death are auspicious, as this had been an old-age practise which is obsolete in modern time practises.

3) POST-DEATH & PRE-CREMATION RITUAL

I) IMMEDIATE POST-DEATH ARRANGEMENTS

a. If death occurs at Home: The deceased's relative should convey the death news to all other close relatives and sadhu or the devotee of the nearby temple.

b. If death occurs in Hospital: Relatives of the deceased should ask the hospital authorities, the time the deceased body will be ready for discharge, so that they can start arranging the final rites for the cremation accordingly.

II) INTERIM DAILY HOME RITUALS

a. In the living room, one should spread a white sheet over a table and place on it a frame/murti of God & picture of the recently deceased. Flowers should be offered to both and a ghee-diva should be kept lit continuously.

b. Each day, an hour or some other fixed amount of time should be spent at the shrine engrossed in singing devotional songs and dhun. The rest of the day a continuous audio-track of a spiritual discourse or dhun should be played-on.

c. When friends or relatives visit, one should try to remain engaged in devotional songs or the spiritual discourse rather than succumb to lamentations or weeping.

d. These above rituals should be performed every day until the body is cremated.

III) PRE-CREMATION PUJA RITUALS

a. As soon as the deceased's body arrives in the home, he/she should be laid on the ground at the prepared spot with the head pointing north.

b. Then the deceased should be covered with a cloth.
   - For male of any age, an unstitched white cloth should be draped over the body as a shroud.
   - For a married woman or a young girl, a sari or a chunri should be used to cover from head to toe.
   - If the deceased is a widow, then she should be covered with a white sari only.

c. The men should sit on one side of the body, and the women should sit on the other side.
   - Arrangements should be made so that the close relatives are able to sit near the body together with respected elders who can console & offer support to the family.

d. All close relatives should gather before the body and recite their own prayers for the beavered soul, and also to avoid the hindrance of any evil element, the **"SHANTIHPATH"** should be recited.

e. A very close relative – eldest son/father/husband/brother should sit on the right side of the body facing south. Have him to take few drops of water in his hand and while holding them, perform the **"SANKALP"**vidhi.
   AUM......season......month......week......date....... day......name of relative performing puja and his relation with the deceased......name of the deceased :- asad-gati-vina shartham......uttam-loka-prapty

*artham……agni-daha-sanskara-nimittam……
mruta-deha-puja   nakhyam……karma   aham
karishye…AUM*

Once finished, have him pour the few drops of water in his hand onto the ground.

f. After Sankalp vidhi the body should be bathed with sanctified water. The bathing rituals should be performed by few close relatives only and others nearby should remain at a distance chanting the spiritual dhun.

g. If circumstances do not permit the body to be bathed, sanctified water should be sprinkled over the body instead.

h. After bathing the body should be dried and dressed.
    • All Male should be dressed/covered with white cloth
    • Women/Girl should be dressed/covered in saree.
    • A widow should be dressed/covered with a plain white saree only.

i. A tulsi leaf along with a drop of sanctified water should be placed in the deceased mouth.

j. AUM, Aum Namah Shivaya or Guru mantra should be chanted in the body's right ear eleven times.

k. A sanctified Kanthi or a double-stringed tulsi bead necklace should be placed around the neck of the deceased. If the deceased used to wear a janoi, then a new janoi should be put on the deceased.

l. Thereafter, male relatives should take turns in applying Chandan-sandalwood paste and a few grains of rice to the deceased forehead followed with placing garland of flowers around the neck of the deceased.

m. Finally, an arti or a small prayer should be performed of the body and then "PUSHPANJALI" – offering flowers on the body by both the male, female and all other close relatives at the feet of the deceased and circumambulating the body simultaneously.

n. Once all these puja rituals are complete, the body should be placed in either a bier or a wooden palanquin. (A bier is usually made of two shafts of bamboo and thirty-two boards, resembling a ladder).

o. The body laid upon a bier should be laid with its face to the sky.

*   The male body should be covered from neck to toe with a white cloth, while the face remains exposed.
*   The female body should be covered with a cloth from head to toe, not keeping the face exposed.

p. A body laid upon a bier should be secured with strings made out of a special kind of grass, called Munj. Alternatively, if such string cannot be found then string made of wool or cotton can be used, then it should be garlanded with flowers and sprinkled with abil & gulal by all the attendees of the funeral.

q. On each of the four corners of the bier, it is customary to tie a coconut and then these are simply placed at the cremation site. (Obsolete symbolic tradition)

4) THE FUNERAL PROCESSION

I) THE RITUAL TIMINGS

The appropriate time for cremation depends on the varying customs of caste, country & tradition. In general, if death occurs during the day time hours, it is preferable for cremation to be carried out that very same day. If death occurs in the evening or at night, cremation is to be carried out the next morning.

II) THE RITUAL FIRE USED FOR CREMATION

a.   The cremation flame should be kindled from dried cow dung in one's home and brought along with the funeral procession in an earthen vessel. A rope should be tied around the neck of the vessel to make a handle and a male representative from the father's side should carry the fire in the funeral procession from home to the cremation grounds.

b.   The relative carrying the flame should walk in front of the bier and no one should come between the bier carrying the body and the relative carrying the fire pot.

III) THOSE CARRYING THE BIER

a.   Only a very close relative, such as an elder son, elder brother, husband etc. should offer their right shoulder to support the front left corner of the bier. The other three corners may be carried by other relatives.

b.   When the bier is leaving the house, the head should exit first (with the deceased face looking towards the house)

c.   Traditionally women should follow the bier as far as the gate of the house. In certain communities, women should follow the procession as far as the village square only.

At that point, water should be sprinkled upon the ground and the bier should be placed at that site so that the women could perform their final circumambulations before returning home. Such practises should be adjusted according to one's respective traditions of place and family.

IV) RITES FOR THE RESTING PLACES ALONG THE FUNERAL PROCESSION

a. A funeral procession makes four stops on its way to the cremation ground.

b. The first stop is on the **verandah of the house**, where the bier is briefly placed on the ground and the procession rests for a moment

c. When the procession reaches the **end of the society of the house**, the bier is set on the ground for a second momentary pause.

d. The third short rest is the spot **between the village outskirts and the cremation ground** or just before entering the gates of the cremation ground. Here when the body is lifted up from the ground, its head should be the first to enter the cremation ground.

e. At the **site of the cremation**, the body should be laid with its head facing south. This is considered the fourth and the final stop of the funeral procession.

5) THE RITES AT THE CREMATORIUM

I) PREPARING THE FUNERAL PYRE

a. In assembling a wood-burning funeral pyre, five to seven thick logs should be laid horizontally in order to create a bier for the body. One split log should be placed directly under the head.

b. Then if available, blades of Durva grass (sacred grass) should be spread atop the pyre. Finally, the body should be untied from the bier and laid on the pyre.

c. The white sheet or blanket covering the body should be removed at this point, but the body should remain otherwise clothed.

d. The eyes, ears, nose, chest, feet and other parts of the body should be anointed with ghee.

e. Split log should be then used to encase the body by placing them in an upside-down "V" over the body so that the resulting fire completely consumes the body. Hay and dried cow dung patties should be used to fill the gaps between the logs. The logs should be arranged such that the face and the toes remain uncovered.

f. Finally, the funeral pyre – known as the **"SMASHANCHITI"** or the **"VEDIKA"** of the **"ANTYESHTI YAGNA"** – is considered ready.

NOTE : Now-a-days due to the Electric crematorium facility, the funeral pyre does not need to be assembled and the mourners can proceed directly to the funeral prayer and rituals prior to cremation.

II) THE FUNERAL PRAYER

a. After assembling the pyre and viewing the deceased for the final time, a short prayer is recited that the soul be blessed with a divine life.

NOTE : The SANKALP, PUJAN, AARTI, PRADAKSHINA & PUSHPANJALI were the funeral prayers which was performed at the house of the deceased followed with the final short prayer (The soul be blessed with a divine life) of the SMASHANCHITI at the **crematorium** just before the pyre is lit or the trolley moves in for the cremation.

III) "AGNIDAAH SANSKAR" – IGNITING THE FUNERAL PYRE

a. A bundle of hay should be ignited with the fire in the earthen pot brought from home and the burning bundle should be handed to the deceased's eldest son, or a close relative.

b. Then holding onto the end of the burning bundle of hay, the person should perform five circumambulations of the pyre, stand facing north and recite a prayer to AGNIDEV or any mantra or just AUM before lighting the funeral pyre at the deceased's head and feet.

c. At the end of each circumambulation, the fire should be touched near the head and feet of the body. At the end of the fifth circumambulation, the entire burning bundle of hay should be placed on the pyre and each plank and blade of grass placed upon the pyre should be lit by the relatives present there-in.

    NOTE : In places where wood-burning cremation is not practiced, the eldest son or a close relative can ignite a stick of incense, circumambulate the casket and the touch the lit incense to each end of the casket to symbolize the traditional Agnidaah ceremony.

d. Once a wood-burning crematory fire has been lit, sesame seeds should be thrown in the fire.

e. Elders and people experienced with cremation should remain present until the body has been completely reduced to ashes.

f. As the crematory fire begins to die down, if certain parts of the body remain unconsumed, ghee, sesame seeds and more split logs can be thrown onto those portions of the pyre to further enkindle the flames so that they consume the entire body.

g. The relatives present should remain until the cremation is complete.

IV) THE FINAL RITES OF BABIES

a. Babies under the age of two are not cremated; rather, they are buried because the delicate bodies of babies are not suited to the harshness of a cremation fire and their life is devoid of sin.

b. Only selective ritual puja is performed, and then, after locating an appropriate, untouched piece of land, the body is buried within a deep grave.

c. To ensure the quickest decomposition and union with the surrounding earth, a large amount of salt should be poured around the body, so that the odor of the decomposing body does not attract anyone or anything, fragrant perfumes should be sprayed around the grave.

d. Additionally, there is no need to carry out many of the Antyeshti rites for such young children.

6) RITUALS AFTER CREMATION

I) RITUALS FOR EXTINGUISHING THE BURNING PYRE

Once the body is completely consumed by the flames, an earthen pot filled with water and some blades of Durva grass and sesame seeds sprinkled into it.

A close relative lifts the pot on his shoulder and stand at the foot of the pyre facing north. Then he uses a small stone to create a hole in the pot. The pot should be positioned so that the stream of water from the hole falls onto the ashes of the deceased's feet.

Then the relatives should circumambulate the pyre allowing the stream of water to flow over the pyre. Then a second hole is created in the pot and another circumambulation is performed. In the same manner the third and fourth holes are made and each should be paired with a circumambulation, allowing the water to flow onto the ashes.

Finally, the pot should be bashed over a rock near the head of the pyre, and the relatives should leave to bathe This ritual is known as **"Cooling of the Ashes"**.

II) COLLECTION & DISPERSAL OF THE ASHES.

Once the pyre has been extinguished, the ashes are collected in a ritual known as **"asthi-sanchayan"**. In Indian towns and cities, small earthen vessels traditionally used to store the ashes are available at the funeral home itself.

If the cremation occurred in a holy place, then the pot of ashes should be immersed in a river, pond, lake, ocean or other sanctified water body at that very site.

If immersion of the ashes in a holy water body is not immediately possible, the pot of ashes should be taken home and should be stored on the terrace of one's home or tied somewhere at external portion of the house or should be kept in any room other than the mandir and the kitchen.

Then, as soon as it is convenient, the ashes should be ceremoniously dispersed in the Ganges or other holy river or water body.

III) POST-CREMATION BATHING

If the funeral home does not have bathing facilities, one should go home, bathe while fully dressed, and only after bathing should one touch anything or anyone at home.

The cremation fire is considered impure. Additionally, dead bodies can be infected with disease. After touching them during the death rites, it is important to remember that germs from the body can ding to the clothes one is wearing and can even spread to other family members. The bathing ritual prevents this from happening.

Scripturally speaking, the ritual sequence after cremation is as follows:

a. **The cremation,**
b. **The ritual bath,**
c. **Darshan of Lord Mahadev (Shiva) at a nearby mandir,**
d. **Chewing a leaf of the neem tree and finally return home.**

Where cremation is done in a funeral home, it is now customary to bathe only after the cremation, cooling of the funeral pyre and the collection of the ashes. After bathing, instead of going to a mandir of Mahadev, friends and relatives proceed to the home of the deceased and offer condolences to the grieving family. Thereafter, everyone returns home.

Generally, no food is cooked at the home of the deceased on the day of the cremation (more specifically, no fire is kindled in the stove, furnace or hearth). Simple food, cooked by other relatives, is brought for the relatives of the deceased. But, in some communities it is permitted to cook a simple meal at the house of the deceased.

IV) PRAYERS FOR THE DECEASED

The family should take solace in performing meritorious deeds on behalf of the departed soul. One can organize prayer assemblies, a series of spiritual discourses, charitable donations and the feeding of sadhus, Brahmins and devotees of God starting from the day following death.

V) COMFORTING THE BEREAVED: THE UTHAMNU OR BESNU

This Custom to provide strength and solace to the bereaved is known as Uthamnu or Besnu. The Uthamnu generally takes place from the second day to the ninth day after death, during which relatives from near and far come to the deceased's home to comfort the deceased's immediate family.

The word uthamnu, literally **'the helping up'**, comes from the idea that after suffering such a devastating loss, family members are broken, and friends and relatives must help them to get back on their feet by being with them in their time of sorrow.

This custom is also known as a Besnu, literally **'the sitting with'**, which describes the friends and family coming home to sit with and offer solace to the bereaved.

VI) OFFERING "SHRANDHANJALI" - THE MEMORIAL SERVICE

In the two to three days after death, the immediate family should inform friends and family about the date, time and location of the memorial service. This service, often called a **Sadadi**, can be held in a community centre or other public place or at one's home.

On the day of the assembly, a white cloth should be spread over a raised platform, or a table or chair on the stage of the venue. Then, a murti or a framed image of one's choicest deity together with a portrait of the recently departed should be placed upon it. Flowers should be placed before the picture of the deceased, and a garland of flowers should be placed around the frame. A stick of incense and a diva should be lit before the images.

As friends and family arrive, they should engage in singing dhun and kirtans. A group of Satsangis or professionals versed in singing devotional songs may also be invited to lead the singing.

Alternatively, an audio track of devotional songs can be played. If possible, sadhus from a nearby Mandir can be invited.

Based on the family's customs and preferences, the assembly should be about an hour or an hour-and-a-half. During this assembly, sadhus and elders should recount the virtues of the deceased.

VII) FUNERAL FEAST & SPONSORING MAHAPUJA – (AN OPTIONAL CUSTOMARY ACT)

After the **Sutak period** - (the period of abstention observed by the Hindus after the death of a family member) is concluded, it is customary to invite virtuous brahmins, sadhus & devotees for a feast or after consulting with local temple sadhus, one may also sponsor **'Mahapuja'**

The other similar act is that on the thirteenth day after death, the family of the deceased may carry out this ritual by performing a small puja in reverence of the departed soul and also by sponsoring a meal to the sadhus, needy and all the near-by relatives. Also, this **13th day** is considered as the last act of concluding all the rituals and the connection between the deceased family and the departed soul. This can be an optional decision as per the situation and the capability of the deceased family and relatives.

VIII) SHAYYA RITUAL: (AN OPTIONAL CUSTOMARY ACT)

On the tenth day after death, the **Shayya ritual** is performed. On this day, new items that the deceased would have liked – such as clothes, shoes, blankets, kitchenware and other household items – are spread on a cot or bed for donating it to a brahmin or the poor and needy.

IX) MARAN SUTAK

During the days of **Sutak** (Ritual cleansing), both male and female relatives wear white clothing which indicates to others that this particular family is observing a period of ritual cleansing.

The Sutak period varied depending on the closeness of the relative - with only one day for very distant relatives and ten days for extremely close relatives.

During these days, one used to have to refrain from performing puja, arti, tilak, mandir darshan, etc.

7) "SHRADDHA"

In Hinduism, **"SHRADDHA"** is a ritual performed by family members in honour of their ancestors, particularly deceased parents. The term **"SHRADDHA"** itself is derived from the root "Shrad," meaning faith. The ritual is deeply rooted in Vedic traditions and is considered a sacred duty to express gratitude and respect to departed souls.

Here's a brief description of the Shraddha ritual in the Hindu Vedic context:

1. **TIMING:** Shraddha is typically performed during the Pitru Paksha, a 16-day lunar period in the Hindu calendar dedicated to honouring ancestors. It usually falls in the Hindu month of Bhadrapada (September– October).

2. **PURPOSE:**
   - **Honoring Ancestors:** The primary purpose of Shraddha is to honour and pay respects to one's ancestors, especially parents and grandparents.
   - **Seeking Blessings:** It is believed that by performing Shraddha rituals, the souls of ancestors receive offerings and blessings, and they, in turn, bless the living.

3. **RITUAL COMPONENTS:**
    - **Tarpana:** Offering water mixed with sesame seeds and barley is done while reciting specific mantras. This is called Tarpana and is meant to satiate the departed souls.
    - **Pinda Daan:** A ball of cooked rice, barley, sesame seeds, and water, known as Pinda, is offered to the ancestors. This act is called Pinda Daan.
    - **Feeding the Brahmins:** Offering food to Brahmins or priests is considered a form of service to ancestors.

4. **LOCATION:** Shraddha rituals are often performed near a water body like a river or a sacred pond, symbolizing the connection between the living and the departed.

5. **MANTRAS AND CHANTS:** Vedic hymns and mantras are recited during the ritual, invoking the blessings of various deities and expressing devotion to the ancestors.

6. **BELIEFS AND SIGNIFICANCE:**
    - **Karmic Balance:** Performing Shraddha is believed to help balance the karmic account of the departed souls, ensuring their well-being in the afterlife.
    - **Ancestral Guidance:** It is believed that honouring ancestors strengthens the bond between the living and the departed, and the ancestors, in turn, guide and protect the family.

7. **CUSTOMS AND PRACTICES:**
   - **Vegetarianism:** It is common for participants to observe vegetarianism on the day of Shraddha.
   - **Clothing:** Participants often wear simple and clean traditional attire during the ritual.
8. **CONCLUDING WITH HOMAM:** In some traditions, the Shraddha ritual is concluded with the performance of a homa (fire ritual) to invoke divine blessings.

Shraddha is a way for Hindu families to express love and gratitude to their ancestors and is deeply ingrained in the cultural and religious fabric of Hinduism. The rituals may vary across regions and communities, but the essence remains the same – a solemn remembrance and homage to the departed souls.

sanskaaram
The Relevance of Vedic Science in Hinduism
A Scientific Approach to "Rituals"
The ABR Concept
(Act, Belief & Relevance)
CONCEPTUALIZED BY:
Ar. K. SHIVKUMAR
pranayugam
A Wellness and Well-being Experiment Based on Vedic Principles
PUSHPANJALI - The Spiritual Intuition Mantra
DHYANAM - The Self Realization Mantra
PRANAYOGAM - The Siddh Vinana Mantra
The '3' Pillars of Life - Spiritual, Mental & Physical
CONCEPTUALIZED BY:
Ar. K. SHIVKUMAR
saptamsidhi
A Vedic Approach to Modern Lifestyle
'A Holistic Concept'
आत्मदीपो भव:
[Be Your Own Light]
CONCEPTUALIZED BY:
Ar. K. SHIVKUMAR
saptagyanam
An Odyssey to the Universal Cosmic Energy (Urja) and its Implications on Human Existence
'An Approach To "PGR" Measures
(Preventive, Guiding & Remedial)
CONCEPTUALIZED BY:
Ar. K. SHIVKUMAR
aarogyaveda
The Vedic and Contemporary Holistic Health Approach for Lifestyle Disorders
An Evaluation of "PST" Measures
(Prevention, Screening & Treatment)
CONCEPTUALIZED BY:
Ar. K. SHIVKUMAR